Fake Refugees

Infiltration of the West

by D.R. Bloor

D.R. Bloor

Copyright © 2024 All rights reserved.

No part of this publication may be reproduced, distributed, or transmitted in any form or by any means, including photocopying, recording, or other electronic or mechanical methods, without the prior written permission of the author, except in the case of brief quotations for academic or critical purposes.

Disclaimer

This book is a work of non-fiction, based on the author's interpretation of current events and publicly available information. The author has made every reasonable effort to ensure the accuracy of the information presented; however, the content should not be taken as definitive or comprehensive. Any resemblance to actual persons, living or dead, or actual events is coincidental. Readers are encouraged to independently verify the information and consult primary sources.

Preface/Author's Note

The topic of immigration is as complex as it is crucial to understanding the dynamics of the modern world. I chose to write this book to delve into two controversial but important issues within immigration policy: the phenomenon of "fake refugees" and the infiltration of foreign agents under the guise of legal immigration. These issues, while uncomfortable, represent significant challenges for Western countries as they navigate the dual goals of humanitarianism and national security.

Believe me when I say that while this book and its content may seem insensitive at some points, it is written by someone who has spent more than 30 years of his life living among refugees and immigrants. I have witnessed the discrimination they face and, on some occasions, experienced it myself. I have seen their struggles, their resilience, and their hopes for a better future. This book is meant to contribute to the safety and well-being of those living a refugee life, the newly legal immigrants, and those now walking toward the European border from the Middle East or making their way to the U.S. border somewhere in the heat of South America.

Consider me a caring, curious average Joe; with that perspective, I have approached these issues objectively, striving to offer readers a balanced view that respects the complexity of the topic. This book is not intended to question the legitimacy of all refugees or immigrants. On the contrary, I firmly believe in the immense contributions that refugees and immigrants make to society and the right of every human being to live in safety and dignity. However, to maintain the integrity of these systems, it is essential to address the instances where they are exploited.

By combining real-life examples, policy discussions, and historical context, my hope is to offer a well-rounded examination of these issues. This book seeks to encourage dialogue, promote fair policies, and strengthen systems in a way that upholds both security and compassion.

Thank you for joining me on this journey into one of the defining challenges of our time.

Dedication

To all those who have been displaced, who seek a better life, and who continue to strive for freedom and dignity despite immense challenges.

To those who are still in the captivity of tyrants, whose courage remains unbroken.

To those who had the chance to flee but chose to stay and fight for justice, knowing they might lose their lives in the process. And to all who work tirelessly to uphold justice, equality, and security for all.

Acknowledgments

This book is the result of years of observing the ever-changing landscape of immigration, integration, and the sociopolitical challenges facing the Western world today. It is born out of a desire to understand the complexities behind migration, to question the often unspoken realities, and to provoke meaningful discussion on how we can protect the values that have made Western countries beacons of hope, opportunity, and freedom.

I wish to express my deepest gratitude to the people who have contributed to my understanding of these pressing issues. To the scholars, journalists, and policy experts whose research and analysis have shed light on the intricacies of immigration systems and the vulnerabilities they face—your work has been invaluable in shaping this book.

I also want to acknowledge the courage of those who have shared their personal stories of migration. Your accounts of struggle, resilience, and hope are powerful reminders of what is at stake in these conversations. They highlight the real human experiences behind the data, bringing context to a topic often reduced to numbers and policies.

I am also grateful to the readers—those who have taken an interest in this book because they care deeply about the future of their communities and the world. I hope this book serves as a catalyst for critical thought, conversation, and change.

Lastly, I acknowledge the values of freedom of speech, democracy, and open discourse that have allowed this book to come to fruition. In a time when many ideas are under threat of censorship or silencing, it is more important than ever to defend our right to explore difficult questions without fear.

May this work contribute in some small way to safeguarding the principles of liberty, equality, and justice that are the bedrock of Western civilization.

Introduction

The global landscape of migration and asylum has evolved dramatically over recent decades. What was once largely a movement driven by wars, natural disasters, and political persecution now includes a complex array of motivations and methods. In many ways, immigration remains the lifeblood of nations, fueling cultural exchange, economic growth, and humanitarian relief. But within this evolving landscape lies a critical issue: how to distinguish between those in genuine need and those who seek to exploit the system.

This book tackles several pressing challenges facing Western immigration systems. First, we explore the phenomenon of fraudulent asylum claims, where individuals—referred to as "fake refugees"—fabricate their backgrounds to gain entry into Western countries. This phenomenon not only undermines the integrity of asylum systems but also places undue strain on resources meant for genuine refugees. Second, we examine how agents of malicious organizations infiltrate Western nations through legal immigration channels. These individuals often represent foreign governments, terrorist networks, or criminal entities, and they enter through various pathways such as investment visas, skilled worker programs, or family reunification. They use their positions to gather intelligence, influence public opinion, or destabilize communities. Third, we delve into the emerging issues around economic refugees and irregular migration, exploring the complex motivations that drive individuals to cross borders in search of a better life.

Throughout this book, we also investigate the broader implications of these issues—from social and economic impacts on host countries to the costs imposed on genuine asylum seekers who face greater scrutiny as a result of fraudulent claims. The book further explores the vulnerabilities within family-based, employment-based, and investment-based immigration pathways, illustrating how each of these channels can be exploited for nefarious purposes. We provide documented case studies to highlight real-life instances of abuse and misuse, shedding light on the strategic goals of those who exploit these systems.

As we delve into these challenges, a key question emerges: How can Western nations uphold their commitments to human rights and humanitarian principles while ensuring their own security? This tension between openness and caution is the foundation of modern immigration policy, and it is a challenge that every nation must navigate with care. To this end, we explore not only the vulnerabilities but also the practical and ethical solutions available—discussing security measures, policy reforms, and innovative approaches aimed at striking the right balance between compassion and caution.

This book is neither a condemnation of migration nor a critique of any particular group. Rather, it is an exploration of the vulnerabilities within immigration systems and a call for improvements that safeguard both national security and the rights of those in need. We recognize the immense contributions of refugees and immigrants to society and affirm the right of every individual to live in safety and dignity. However, in order to maintain the integrity of these systems, it is crucial to address the instances where they are exploited.

By combining real-life examples, policy discussions, and historical context, my hope is to offer a well-rounded examination of these issues. We aim to present a balanced view, examining documented cases, analyzing their impacts on genuine refugees, and reviewing the policy measures that nations have implemented in response. We also delve into broader topics, such as the social and economic costs of immigration fraud, and propose thoughtful reforms and effective policies that can lead to immigration systems that are both compassionate and secure.

As we begin this journey, I invite readers to approach these topics with an open mind. The goal is not to discourage migration or cast suspicion on newcomers but to better understand the complexities of a system that affects millions of lives worldwide. With thoughtful reforms and effective policies, we can build immigration systems that protect national security, uphold humanitarian commitments, and foster communities that thrive on diversity.

Table of Contents

Part I: Understanding and Exploiting the Refugee System

Chapter One: Understanding the Refugee System

This chapter introduces the basic framework of refugee and asylum systems, helping readers understand the foundation upon which later discussions will build.

Introduction

The international refugee system is built on a foundation of humanitarian principles, designed to protect those who face persecution, violence, and existential threats in their home countries. It seeks to offer refuge and safety to the world's most vulnerable populations. With roots in the aftermath of World War II, when nations came together to establish international protections for displaced people, the system has grown and evolved over the decades. However, it has also become more complex, as the forces driving migration have diversified and increased in scale.

In this chapter, we explore how the refugee system functions, including the processes and standards that govern it. Understanding this framework is essential for examining how some individuals exploit the system and how genuine refugees are affected as a result. As we delve into the system's strengths and vulnerabilities, we lay the groundwork for understanding the dual challenges of maintaining security and protecting human rights in today's migration landscape.

The Refugee Status Determination Process

The process of determining refugee status, often referred to as **Refugee Status Determination (RSD)**, is a critical part of the asylum system. This process is the mechanism by which authorities decide if an individual meets the criteria to be granted asylum. The key international guideline for defining a refugee is the **1951 Refugee Convention**, which specifies that a refugee is someone who has a well-founded fear of persecution due to race, religion, nationality, membership in a particular social group, or political opinion. This convention, along with its 1967 Protocol, serves as the basis for most national refugee policies.

RSD is typically conducted by trained officers or judges who interview applicants, review evidence, and make judgments on whether their cases meet the established criteria. The process varies between countries, but it generally involves an initial application, followed by interviews and assessments. If applicants are found to meet the criteria, they may be granted refugee status, which allows them to stay in the host country legally and receive support.

While this system is intended to ensure that only those with genuine claims are protected, it is also inherently complex. It relies heavily on the applicant's ability to convey their story, provide documentation (which is often difficult or impossible to obtain in dangerous situations), and navigate legal processes in an unfamiliar country.

Criteria for Refugee Status and Asylum

To qualify as a refugee, an individual must meet specific criteria, primarily focused on the threat of persecution. According to the **UN Refugee Agency (UNHCR)**, asylum seekers must demonstrate a credible fear of returning to their home country due to one of the five grounds listed in the 1951 Refugee Convention. However, proving persecution can be challenging, as it often involves subjective judgments about credibility and risk. This can lead to disparities in how different countries interpret the same criteria.

For instance, persecution might include threats of violence, imprisonment, torture, or discrimination that severely limits a person's rights. However, individuals fleeing generalized violence, poverty, or environmental disasters often do not qualify under these criteria, even if they face significant hardship. This has led to debates about whether the definition of "refugee" should be expanded to include individuals fleeing these situations.

In addition to meeting the persecution criteria, asylum seekers must also demonstrate that they are unable to find protection within their home country. This is known as the **principle of "unable or unwilling protection"** and is a crucial part of the refugee framework. It requires applicants to show that their home government cannot or will not protect them from persecution, making it necessary for them to seek refuge abroad.

Agencies and International Agreements Involved

The global refugee system operates through a network of international organizations, national governments, and non-governmental organizations (NGOs). The **UN Refugee Agency**

(UNHCR) is the primary organization overseeing refugee protections. Established in 1950, UNHCR works to support refugees through assistance programs, advocacy, and coordination of international responses. The agency also collaborates with countries to uphold the principles of the 1951 Refugee Convention and ensure compliance with international standards.

In addition to UNHCR, there are numerous international agreements and organizations involved in refugee protection. These include regional agreements like the **Dublin Regulation in the European Union**, which sets out guidelines for handling asylum applications within EU countries. Other agreements, such as the **Cartagena Declaration on Refugees** in Latin America and the **Organization of African Unity's Convention Governing the Specific Aspects of Refugee Problems in Africa**, broaden the definition of refugee to include individuals fleeing violence and other crises that may not be covered under the 1951 Convention.

National governments play a key role in enforcing these international standards through their own asylum laws and procedures. However, the interpretation and application of refugee law can vary widely between countries. Some nations implement more restrictive policies, while others adopt a more open approach. This inconsistency creates disparities in how refugees are treated and can result in "asylum shopping," where individuals seek out countries with more favorable policies.

Challenges in the Modern Refugee System

While the refugee system has provided critical protections to millions of people worldwide, it also faces significant challenges. One major issue is the sheer scale of displacement in the modern era. According to UNHCR, more than 100 million people are forcibly displaced globally, with a growing number seeking asylum in Western countries. This has placed immense pressure on national asylum systems, leading to long wait times, resource shortages, and public concerns over immigration.

Another challenge lies in the nature of modern conflicts and crises. Today, displacement is often driven by a complex mix of factors, including poverty, climate change, organized crime, and civil unrest. Many people do not meet the strict definition of "refugee" under the 1951 Convention, even though they face real dangers. This creates difficult ethical questions about who should receive protection and highlights the limitations of the current system in addressing modern migration dynamics.

Finally, the refugee system is vulnerable to exploitation by individuals who may not have legitimate claims. Fraudulent applications, identity manipulation, and fabricated stories can undermine public trust in the system and strain resources meant for genuine refugees. In subsequent chapters, we'll explore how these issues manifest and examine potential solutions that protect both the integrity of the system and the rights of those who need it most.

Conclusion

The international refugee system is a vital part of the global response to human rights abuses and displacement. It offers hope and safety to millions, yet it faces challenges in addressing both the scale and complexity of modern migration. As we move forward in this book, we'll delve deeper into the vulnerabilities within this system, exploring how certain individuals exploit these weaknesses and examining the consequences for genuine refugees.

By understanding the foundations and challenges of the refugee system, readers will be better equipped to explore the delicate balance between security and humanitarianism that lies at the heart of modern immigration debates.

Chapter Two: Vulnerabilities in the System

This chapter will delve into the specific vulnerabilities that can be exploited within refugee and asylum processes. This chapter will outline common types of fraud and manipulation within the refugee system, exploring why these vulnerabilities exist and how they impact both the system itself and those it's designed to protect.

Introduction

The refugee and asylum system is designed to offer protection to those who have nowhere else to turn, a safe haven for individuals escaping persecution, conflict, and danger. However, like any large and complex system, it is not immune to exploitation. Some individuals, driven by economic motives or other personal incentives, attempt to enter the system under false pretenses, claiming asylum with fabricated stories, manipulated documents, or altered identities. While these cases represent a small percentage of overall claims, they can have a disproportionate impact on public perception and strain resources intended for those in genuine need.

This chapter examines the vulnerabilities in the asylum process that allow some to exploit it. From fraudulent documents to identity manipulation and false narratives, we'll explore the common methods used to deceive the system, why these gaps exist, and the broader consequences of these actions on the integrity of the refugee system.

Common Forms of Fraud in Asylum Claims

Fraudulent activities in the asylum process vary widely in scope and sophistication. Some individuals may exaggerate the level of threat they face, while others go to great lengths to create entirely fabricated stories of persecution. Understanding the different forms of fraud is key to recognizing where and why the system fails to detect these abuses.

1. **Document Forgery and Falsification**

   Document forgery is one of the most prevalent forms of fraud within asylum applications. Applicants may submit falsified passports, birth certificates, and other identification documents that support their claims of persecution or obscure their true identity. In some cases, individuals may forge documents to alter their nationality, creating a narrative of fleeing a specific conflict or persecution associated with a particular country or region. Because many asylum seekers come from areas with limited bureaucratic infrastructure, verifying the authenticity of foreign documents can be challenging for immigration authorities.

Example: In cases involving conflict zones where record-keeping is minimal or non-existent, applicants might present forged papers showing citizenship in a conflict-ridden country to bolster their asylum claims. These forgeries can be difficult to detect, especially if verification systems are weak or authorities lack access to reliable databases in those regions.

2. **Identity Manipulation and Multiple Applications**

   Identity manipulation occurs when an individual uses multiple identities to submit asylum applications in various countries or regions. This is often done to increase the chances of approval or to exploit differences in asylum policies across borders. By using different names or altering birth dates and family histories, some applicants can submit several claims, hoping that at least one will be accepted. Identity fraud may also involve using another person's identification, effectively stealing their identity to obtain asylum.

Example: Reports indicate that certain asylum seekers have applied under different names in multiple European Union countries, a practice known as "asylum shopping." This tactic is used to avoid detection, as each application is filed separately in hopes that no cross-checking will occur.

3. **Fabricated Narratives of Persecution**
   Some applicants create entirely fabricated stories to present themselves as victims of persecution. In these cases, the narrative might include tales of political repression, religious discrimination, or threats of violence that did not actually occur. False narratives are particularly difficult to detect, as they rely heavily on the applicant's testimony and are often based on generalized, unverifiable claims of abuse.

Example: An applicant might claim to belong to a persecuted minority in their home country, detailing incidents of harassment, threats, or violence that cannot be easily verified by immigration authorities. Without clear evidence to confirm or refute these claims, asylum officers face a significant challenge in making an accurate assessment.

4. **False Claims of Family Relationships**
   Another vulnerability in the asylum system lies in family reunification policies, which allow immediate family members of recognized refugees to join them in the host country. Some individuals exploit this provision by falsely claiming familial relationships with refugees, either through fraudulent documents or verbal claims. This is particularly common in cases where a recognized refugee will vouch for a friend or distant relative, who then claims to be a close family member to gain entry.

Example: In countries with strong family reunification policies, applicants might present forged marriage certificates or claim children who are not biologically theirs. By passing these individuals off as immediate family members, they can secure a pathway to residency without direct verification.

Why These Vulnerabilities Exist

The reasons for these vulnerabilities are complex and multifaceted. They stem from the inherent challenges in processing high volumes of asylum claims, the limited resources available to immigration authorities, and the often opaque nature of international document verification. Here are some key factors that contribute to these gaps in the system:

1. **High Volume of Applications**
   Western countries, particularly those in Europe and North America, receive thousands of asylum applications each year. The sheer volume of these applications can overwhelm the resources available to process them, resulting in rushed or incomplete evaluations. As a result, some fraudulent claims slip through, as officers may not

have the time or capacity to conduct thorough investigations for each case.

2. **Limited Access to Reliable Verification Databases**
   Verifying the authenticity of foreign documents is a significant challenge for immigration authorities. Countries in conflict zones or under authoritarian rule may not maintain reliable identification records, or they may be unwilling to share information with foreign governments. Without access to accurate databases, it becomes difficult for authorities to determine if a passport, birth certificate, or other documentation is genuine.

3. **Inconsistent International Cooperation**
   Effective asylum processing often requires international cooperation. However, political considerations, resource disparities, and differing national interests can hinder cooperation across borders. For example, some countries may refuse to cooperate on security grounds, limiting the exchange of information that could help identify fraudulent cases. This lack of coordination creates opportunities for individuals to exploit inconsistencies between nations.

4. **Humanitarian Mandate and Ethical Constraints**
   The humanitarian focus of the refugee system also plays a role in creating vulnerabilities. Asylum officers are trained to approach cases with empathy and sensitivity, prioritizing the protection of individuals who may have experienced severe trauma. This compassionate approach, while essential for helping genuine refugees, can also make it easier for fraud to go undetected, as

officers may be reluctant to question or challenge applicants who appear vulnerable.

Impact of Fraud on the Asylum System and Genuine Refugees

Fraudulent claims are more than just administrative problems; they have real and significant impacts on the asylum system and on individuals seeking genuine protection. The consequences of fraud affect various aspects of the system, leading to delays, resource strains, and shifts in public perception.

1. **Increased Processing Times and Resource Strain**
   Fraudulent claims contribute to the backlog of asylum cases, resulting in longer wait times for everyone involved. This can delay critical assistance for genuine refugees, who may be left in limbo for months or even years. As resources are diverted to investigate questionable claims, genuine applicants suffer from slower processing and fewer support services.

2. **Negative Public Perception of Refugees**
   When high-profile cases of asylum fraud come to light, they can influence public opinion, leading to increased skepticism toward refugees in general. This can create a culture of mistrust, making it harder for genuine refugees to be welcomed and supported in host countries. Media coverage of fraud cases can also lead to calls for stricter immigration policies, which may inadvertently impact legitimate refugees.

3. **Policy Shifts Toward Restriction**
   In response to cases of fraud, governments may adopt more restrictive asylum policies, implementing stricter

verification procedures or limiting the grounds for asylum. While these policies are intended to prevent abuse, they often make the system more challenging for legitimate refugees, who may struggle to meet the increased demands for documentation or detailed personal histories.

4. **Increased Scrutiny on All Asylum Seekers**

    Fraud cases create a ripple effect, leading to more intense scrutiny of all asylum seekers. Genuine refugees may face additional questioning, skepticism, and invasive processes that can be retraumatizing, particularly if they have fled severe persecution. This heightened scrutiny can make the process more difficult for vulnerable individuals who lack the resources to navigate complex immigration systems.

Conclusion

The vulnerabilities in the asylum system present significant challenges for governments, genuine refugees, and the public. While the majority of asylum seekers have valid claims, the existence of fraud creates a complex landscape that requires careful navigation. In the following chapters, we will examine real-life examples of fraud, analyze their impacts, and explore potential solutions that balance compassion with security. The goal is to create a system that protects those in need while minimizing opportunities for exploitation.

Chapter Three: Real-Life Case Studies

This chapter will explore documented examples of asylum fraud and exploitation, providing real-life illustrations of the issues discussed in previous chapters. By examining these cases, we can better understand the practical impact of fraud on the asylum system and the challenges authorities face in distinguishing genuine refugees from those with fabricated claims.

Introduction

The abstract concepts of asylum fraud and immigration exploitation become clearer through specific, real-life examples. Documented cases of fraud within asylum systems reveal the lengths to which some individuals go to manipulate the system, as well as the real consequences of these actions. While these cases may represent a minority of asylum applications, they often attract significant attention due to their impact on resources, public opinion, and policy. In this chapter, we will examine a selection of real-life cases that illustrate various forms of fraud, from fabricated identities to exploitation of family reunification policies. These cases demonstrate the challenges faced by immigration authorities and highlight the need for a balanced, vigilant approach to asylum processing.

Case Study 1: Multiple Identities and Asylum Shopping in Europe

One notable example of asylum fraud involves the tactic known as **asylum shopping**—the practice of applying for asylum in multiple countries under different identities to increase the chances of approval. This method has been reported across Europe, particularly among applicants from countries with high volumes of asylum seekers. Asylum shopping not only strains the resources of multiple countries but also undermines the integrity of international asylum systems.

Background: In one case that received significant media attention, an individual from North Africa applied for asylum in several European countries, including Germany, France, and Belgium, under different names and backgrounds. By altering his identity and fabricating stories of persecution, he was able to receive temporary protection in some countries while reapplying in others when his status was challenged or revoked.

Methods Used: The individual took advantage of Europe's decentralized asylum processing system, where each country manages its own asylum applications. He obtained forged documents and created multiple identities, each with unique backgrounds and personal histories. Because he applied in separate countries, it was difficult for authorities to detect his fraud, as there was limited data-sharing among the asylum systems of each nation at the time.

Consequences and Repercussions: Eventually, authorities uncovered the deception when biometric data cross-checking exposed his multiple identities. This case led to increased scrutiny on applicants, delays in processing times for others, and a policy shift toward stricter verification methods. It also contributed to calls for improved data-sharing across EU countries to prevent similar incidents in the future.

Case Study 2: Document Forgery and False Narratives in the United States

Document forgery is a common form of asylum fraud, particularly among applicants who come from regions with limited or unreliable record-keeping. In the United States, one well-publicized case involved an individual from Eastern Europe who fabricated an elaborate story of political persecution, supported by falsified documents.

Background: This individual claimed to be an activist persecuted by the government in his home country for participating in anti-regime protests. His asylum application included forged documents purportedly issued by his government, including arrest warrants, legal summons, and even a falsified newspaper article reporting his "arrest."

Methods Used: He worked with a network of document forgers who specialized in creating realistic government documents. By presenting these as evidence, he strengthened his narrative of persecution, which would have been difficult to prove otherwise. His detailed, well-crafted story and supporting documents initially convinced U.S. immigration officials of the validity of his claims.

Consequences and Repercussions: The fraud was discovered after a routine background check revealed inconsistencies in his story, leading to further investigation. Authorities later found that he was part of a larger network involved in asylum fraud, with connections to multiple individuals who were using similar forged documents. This case heightened awareness within U.S. immigration services of the risks associated with document forgery, resulting in increased funding for verification technology and more rigorous background checks for applicants from high-risk regions.

Case Study 3: Family Reunification Exploitation in Canada

Family reunification policies are intended to support refugees by allowing close family members to join them in the host country. However, these policies are sometimes exploited by individuals who falsely claim familial relationships to gain entry. In Canada, one case exposed a scheme in which individuals posed as family members of recognized refugees, taking advantage of the reunification policy to gain residency.

Background: In this case, a man from a conflict-affected country gained refugee status in Canada, and subsequently filed family reunification applications for his "wife" and "children." Upon arrival, however, authorities noticed discrepancies in the ages and identification documents of the individuals who claimed to be his family. Further investigation revealed that none of the people listed were biologically related to him; they were, in fact, acquaintances from his home country who paid him to vouch for them.

Methods Used: The man had obtained forged marriage and birth certificates to present the group as a family unit. He provided the necessary documentation, which appeared legitimate at first glance, and coached his supposed "family members" on their backstory to ensure their responses matched during interviews with Canadian immigration officials.

Consequences and Repercussions: When the fraud was exposed, it led to policy changes in Canada's family reunification procedures, including stricter scrutiny of familial claims and mandatory DNA testing in cases where documentation was unreliable or inconclusive. This case highlighted the need for better verification methods in family reunification programs, as well as the vulnerability of such programs to exploitation by those seeking a shortcut to residency.

Case Study 4: Economic Fraud and Exploiting Humanitarian Grounds in the United Kingdom

Economic migration—while legitimate in many contexts—does not typically qualify an individual for asylum under international standards. However, some applicants attempt to use fabricated claims of persecution as a means to secure asylum for economic reasons. In the United Kingdom, one case involved a man from a stable, non-conflict country who claimed asylum based on a fabricated story of religious persecution.

Background: The man applied for asylum, stating that he was a member of a persecuted religious minority in his home country. He claimed that he faced threats and discrimination, which left him with no choice but to flee. However, background checks revealed that he had no prior affiliation with the religious group he claimed to belong to and that he had been economically motivated, seeking a better life for himself and his family.

Methods Used: The applicant presented a well-constructed story of hardship, supported by testimonials from individuals who were part of his "religious community." He had no prior record of practicing the religion, nor any evidence of involvement with the community. This raised suspicions, leading immigration officials to dig deeper into his background and uncover the inconsistencies in his claim.

Consequences and Repercussions: The discovery of fraud led to stricter requirements for asylum claims based on religious persecution, including verification of religious affiliation in applicants' home countries. This case underscored the challenge of distinguishing economic migrants from genuine refugees, particularly when the applicants present compelling but fabricated stories.

Case Study 5: Agents of Malicious Organizations in Legal Immigration Pathways

Not all fraudulent asylum claims are based on individual motives; some are part of orchestrated efforts by organizations to infiltrate a country. In one instance, members of a foreign government's intelligence network entered a Western country as refugees, using fabricated claims of persecution to avoid detection.

Background: The individuals, who later admitted to working for a foreign intelligence agency, claimed to be dissidents fleeing persecution. They used the asylum system to gain entry, intending to establish a network and conduct intelligence operations. Their application included fabricated documents that portrayed them as political activists, and they took advantage of the host country's expedited asylum procedures for individuals claiming imminent danger.

Methods Used: By posing as political refugees, they were able to avoid the background checks typically associated with other visa types. They were well-prepared, presenting forged arrest records and letters from fictitious human rights organizations to support their story. Once granted asylum, they began carrying out intelligence operations, using their protected status to avoid scrutiny.

Consequences and Repercussions: When the scheme was uncovered, it led to international tensions and a thorough review of asylum processes in the host country. It also prompted the introduction of stricter checks for applicants from regions associated with state-sponsored espionage, as well as increased collaboration between immigration services and intelligence agencies.

Conclusion

These case studies provide a window into the complex challenges that asylum systems face. While the majority of asylum seekers are individuals fleeing genuine persecution, these examples demonstrate how vulnerabilities in the system can be exploited. Fraudulent cases not only divert resources away from genuine refugees but also impact public perception, fueling skepticism and calls for restrictive policies.

The cases examined in this chapter highlight the importance of vigilance, comprehensive verification processes, and international cooperation in maintaining the integrity of asylum systems. As we continue, the book will address policy measures that aim to curb such abuses, exploring solutions that protect both national security and the rights of those in true need of protection.

Chapter Four: Impact on Genuine Refugees

This chapter will focus on the broad and specific ways in which fraudulent asylum claims impact genuine refugees, including increased scrutiny, resource strain, and negative public perception. Additionally, it will cover cases of individuals who return to their countries of origin after obtaining citizenship, a practice that raises questions about the validity of some asylum claims and leads to more restrictive policies for all applicants.

Introduction

The asylum system is a lifeline for individuals fleeing persecution, war, and other forms of oppression. Yet, when this system is manipulated by those with fraudulent claims, the consequences extend far beyond isolated cases of abuse. Fraudulent asylum claims place undue pressure on the system, divert resources, and strain the public's trust in immigration processes. For genuine refugees, the effects of these challenges are profound, as they face longer processing times, increased scrutiny, and harsher policies.

This chapter examines how fraudulent practices in the asylum process harm genuine refugees. We will delve into the various ways in which fraud leads to public skepticism, encourages restrictive policies, and ultimately makes it more difficult for those in true need to receive timely protection. Additionally, we will explore cases where individuals, after obtaining citizenship, have returned to their countries of origin—an act that often raises questions about the legitimacy of some asylum claims. This behavior fuels further doubts and complicates the situation for genuine refugees, who depend on the integrity and compassion of the asylum system.

Increased Scrutiny and Administrative Burden

One of the most immediate impacts of asylum fraud is the increased administrative burden it places on the immigration system. Processing fraudulent claims requires additional verification measures, and the time and resources spent investigating these claims slow down the entire process, creating delays that affect genuine applicants.

1. **Processing Delays**

   Immigration authorities in many Western countries are already overwhelmed by high volumes of asylum applications. When fraudulent claims are added to the mix, it increases the backlog of cases, extending wait times for all applicants. For genuine refugees, who are often in dire need of safety and stability, these delays can mean prolonged periods of uncertainty, detention, or temporary housing that may be far from ideal. In some cases, families remain separated as they await processing, with children left in unstable or unsafe situations.

2. **Stricter Verification Requirements**

   Due to cases of fraud, immigration authorities have had to implement more rigorous verification procedures. These might include requiring additional documentation, performing in-depth background checks, and conducting repeated interviews to assess credibility. For genuine refugees, who may be fleeing dangerous circumstances without access to personal documents, meeting these increased requirements can be a significant challenge. Refugees who have experienced trauma may also struggle with the repeated questioning or demands for evidence, which can feel invasive or retraumatizing.

3. **Example: Backlog in the European Asylum System**
Europe has faced significant backlogs in its asylum processing due to an influx of applications, particularly since the Syrian refugee crisis. In countries like Germany, where applications increased rapidly, fraudulent claims from individuals posing as Syrians were reported. This added to delays, as authorities had to sift through claims to distinguish genuine refugees from those attempting to exploit the crisis. Genuine refugees faced extended wait times as a result, with some waiting years for their applications to be processed.

Negative Public Perception and Its Consequences

Asylum fraud has a significant impact on public perception, often fostering mistrust and resentment toward refugees as a whole. When instances of fraud are highlighted in the media, they tend to overshadow the vast majority of genuine cases, skewing public perception and leading to greater skepticism of asylum seekers. This negative perception can have far-reaching consequences for the support and resources available to genuine refugees.

1. **Influence on Public Opinion**
High-profile cases of asylum fraud tend to receive substantial media coverage, which shapes public opinion. When people perceive that the asylum system is easily

exploited, support for refugee programs declines. Host communities may become more resistant to welcoming newcomers, assuming that a significant portion of asylum seekers are insincere. This shift in public opinion makes it harder for genuine refugees to integrate into society, as they may face hostility or suspicion from local populations.

2. **Political Pressure and Policy Shifts**

   Negative public opinion often leads to increased political pressure on governments to restrict asylum policies. Policymakers may respond by implementing tougher criteria for asylum, intensifying screening processes, or even reducing quotas for asylum admissions. For genuine refugees, these policy shifts mean additional barriers to securing protection. In some cases, restrictive policies may require more extensive proof of persecution or limit access to legal assistance, further complicating the path to safety for those fleeing dangerous conditions.

3. **Media Coverage of Fraud Cases**

   Media outlets often prioritize sensational stories, and cases of asylum fraud can attract significant attention. This coverage paints a distorted picture, making it seem as though fraud is rampant within the asylum system. Stories of individuals who falsified persecution claims or manipulated the system are widely reported, while the majority of genuine cases go unnoticed. This focus on fraud cases creates an environment in which refugees are viewed with suspicion, complicating the process of building trust with host communities.

Policy Changes in Response to Fraud

Governments worldwide have responded to asylum fraud by enacting policies aimed at preventing abuse. While these measures are necessary to maintain the system's integrity, they often come at a cost to genuine refugees, who must navigate increasingly complex and restrictive procedures to prove their eligibility. These policy shifts reflect the challenges governments face in balancing security with humanitarian obligations.

1. **Cessation Hearings**
   Canada has implemented a policy of cessation hearings, where authorities can revoke refugee status or citizenship if evidence arises that an individual has misrepresented their need for protection. This process allows Canada to address cases of fraud, particularly when individuals return to their countries of origin after claiming persecution. While this policy helps reduce abuse, it also places an additional burden on genuine refugees, who may need to prove their ongoing need for protection to avoid scrutiny.

2. **Stricter Documentation Requirements**
   In response to fraud, countries such as Germany, France, and the United States have increased documentation requirements for asylum applicants. Genuine refugees, however, may not have access to the necessary documents, as conflict or persecution often forces them to flee without paperwork. In some instances, refugees are unable to meet the new requirements due to a lack of infrastructure in their home countries, where record-keeping may be minimal or unreliable.

3. **Expanded Investigative Measures**

   To prevent fraud, some countries have introduced enhanced investigative practices, including monitoring social media accounts, tracking travel history, and conducting more intensive background checks. While these measures help identify fraudulent claims, they also place legitimate refugees under increased surveillance. Genuine applicants may feel that they are treated with suspicion and subject to scrutiny that complicates their transition to safety and stability.

Returning to Country of Origin Post-Citizenship

One of the more complex aspects of asylum fraud is the trend of refugees returning to their home countries after obtaining citizenship in their host country. This behavior often raises questions about the authenticity of initial asylum claims, as returning to a place supposedly deemed unsafe may suggest that the danger was either exaggerated or fabricated. This issue has been observed in several Western countries and has led to increased scrutiny of refugees who travel to their countries of origin.

1. **Pattern of Return Travel**

   This pattern of return travel is notable in several countries, including Canada, the United States, and the European Union. Some individuals, after obtaining citizenship and the rights it entails, return to the countries they initially claimed were unsafe. While there may be legitimate reasons for return travel—such as family emergencies or personal obligations—frequent or prolonged visits can raise doubts about the original claims of persecution. Immigration authorities have had to weigh these cases carefully, as return travel can indicate that an individual no longer requires protection.

- **Canada**: Canada has faced cases of individuals from Iran, Syria, and other regions returning home shortly after obtaining Canadian citizenship. Canada's response has included initiating cessation hearings, where authorities can revoke refugee status if it's found that an individual no longer faces danger in their home country. These cases have contributed to public skepticism and have prompted policy discussions on how to manage return travel among refugees.

- **European Union**: EU member states like Germany and Sweden have also observed instances where refugees from Iraq, Afghanistan, and Syria return to their countries of origin. Some governments have responded by implementing policies that allow for the revocation of refugee status if the individual's return indicates that they no longer require protection. These measures aim to prevent exploitation while ensuring that the system serves those in genuine need.

- **United States**: In the United States, instances of refugees from countries like Iraq and Somalia returning home have led to increased scrutiny by the Department of Homeland Security (DHS) and U.S. Citizenship and Immigration Services (USCIS). Some cases have prompted investigations to determine whether applicants' initial claims of persecution were valid. This has reinforced the importance of the "intent to permanently reside" requirement in U.S. citizenship and asylum applications.

2. **Impact on Public Trust and Refugee Programs**

   When cases of post-citizenship return travel are revealed, they often damage public trust in refugee programs. Citizens begin to question whether asylum systems are adequately verifying claims, which can lead to calls for more restrictive policies and even reduced support for refugee initiatives. This erosion of public trust affects genuine refugees, as they may encounter increased skepticism and resentment within host communities.

3. **Consequences for Genuine Refugees**

   Genuine refugees, who may eventually wish to return to their home countries when conditions improve, are often impacted by these cases. Return travel is sometimes necessary for refugees with close family ties or other personal obligations, yet they face heightened scrutiny and questioning, even if their intentions are legitimate. This increased oversight can be re-traumatizing and make it difficult for refugees to navigate the already challenging process of integrating into a new society.

Conclusion

The impact of fraudulent asylum claims extends beyond individual cases, affecting the entire asylum system and those who genuinely need protection. Fraudulent cases place strain on administrative resources, foster public skepticism, and lead to more restrictive policies. The issue of refugees returning to their countries of origin after gaining citizenship is particularly damaging, as it raises questions about the authenticity of initial claims and fuels public distrust.

As asylum systems adapt to address these challenges, the need for balanced, thoughtful policies remains essential. While it is necessary to safeguard the system from exploitation, it is equally important to uphold the rights and dignity of genuine refugees, who depend on the integrity and compassion of their host countries

Chapter Five: Policy Responses and Reforms

This chapter will discuss various policy measures that countries have implemented to address vulnerabilities in the asylum system. This chapter will explore how these policies aim to prevent fraud while balancing humanitarian responsibilities. We'll cover reforms that enhance security measures, promote transparency, and strengthen the asylum system without unduly burdening genuine refugees.

Introduction

Addressing fraud and exploitation within the asylum system is a complex challenge, as it requires a careful balance between security and compassion. Governments worldwide are under pressure to respond to instances of asylum abuse by implementing policies that prevent fraud while maintaining accessibility for those who truly need protection. This chapter explores a range of policy responses and reforms that countries have enacted to preserve the integrity of their asylum systems, minimize abuse, and improve the efficiency of processing applications.

From biometric verification systems to data-sharing agreements, these policies represent a concerted effort to identify fraudulent claims while ensuring that genuine refugees are not unduly affected. We will examine specific policies from countries such as Canada, the United States, and the European Union, and analyze their effectiveness, challenges, and impact on both fraud prevention and the asylum experience for legitimate refugees.

Enhanced Screening and Verification Measures

One of the primary responses to asylum fraud has been the implementation of enhanced screening and verification measures. These measures aim to verify applicants' identities, assess the credibility of their claims, and prevent fraudulent entries into the asylum system. Advances in technology have facilitated more thorough screenings, although these measures come with challenges, especially for refugees who may lack documentation due to conflict or persecution.

1. **Biometric Identification**

   Many countries have introduced biometric identification as a means of verifying the identities of asylum seekers. Biometric data, including fingerprints, facial recognition, and iris scans, provides a reliable way to identify individuals and prevent multiple applications under different identities. This technology has been adopted widely within the European Union through the Eurodac system, which allows member states to share and cross-check biometric data on asylum seekers.

Example: Eurodac is a centralized European database that stores fingerprint data for all asylum seekers over the age of 14. This system helps prevent "asylum shopping" by allowing authorities to track where applicants have previously filed claims. If an individual applies for asylum in multiple EU countries, Eurodac can identify them, ensuring that their application is processed only once within the EU framework.

2. **Document Verification and Forgery Detection**

   Given the prevalence of document forgery, countries have implemented sophisticated verification processes to assess the authenticity of passports, birth certificates, and other identification documents submitted by asylum seekers. Technology such as ultraviolet scanners and digital forensics helps detect forged documents, reducing the likelihood of fraudulent claims based on altered identities or fabricated backgrounds.

Example: Canada's Immigration, Refugees, and Citizenship Canada (IRCC) has invested in high-tech scanners and training for officers to identify forged documents. The IRCC has established partnerships with agencies in other countries to exchange knowledge and technology, allowing for more effective detection of document fraud.

3. **Expanded Interview Techniques and Psychological Assessments**

   Some countries have introduced expanded interview protocols, including training for officers on how to detect signs of deception. Enhanced interview techniques include analyzing inconsistencies in applicants' stories, assessing cultural knowledge, and, in some cases, conducting psychological assessments. These measures can help differentiate genuine refugees from individuals presenting fabricated stories.

Example: The U.S. Department of Homeland Security (DHS) has implemented interview protocols designed to detect inconsistencies in asylum applications. Officers receive specialized training to ask probing questions and assess credibility through both verbal and non-verbal cues. In cases where psychological trauma may influence an applicant's responses, officers work with mental health professionals to ensure a fair evaluation.

Data Sharing and International Cooperation

International cooperation and data-sharing agreements have become essential components in preventing asylum fraud. By sharing information across borders, countries can better identify individuals attempting to exploit asylum systems, ensure consistent processing, and streamline application procedures. Data-sharing initiatives help prevent "asylum shopping" and reduce the likelihood of individuals making fraudulent claims in multiple countries.

1. **Data-Sharing Agreements between Countries**
   Data-sharing agreements allow countries to access information about asylum seekers, including biometric data, travel history, and previous asylum applications. These agreements help prevent individuals from submitting multiple applications in different countries and facilitate the identification of known fraudsters or individuals associated with criminal organizations.

Example: The **Five Eyes Alliance**, comprising the United States, Canada, the United Kingdom, Australia, and New Zealand, has established a data-sharing agreement for immigration and security purposes. Through this agreement, member countries share information about individuals seeking asylum, including biometric data and any criminal records. This cooperation helps prevent individuals with fraudulent histories or criminal associations from entering the system in multiple countries.

2. **Cross-Border Intelligence Collaboration**
   In addition to sharing data on asylum seekers, countries have strengthened intelligence collaboration to identify potential threats associated with asylum fraud. Intelligence agencies monitor known individuals affiliated with terrorist organizations or criminal networks and share relevant information with immigration authorities. This approach allows for early detection of individuals attempting to misuse the asylum system for infiltration or criminal activities.

Example: In the European Union, Europol collaborates with Frontex (the European Border and Coast Guard Agency) to monitor asylum seekers who may be associated with criminal or terrorist organizations. Europol shares intelligence reports with EU member states, providing information on high-risk individuals who may attempt to exploit asylum channels for entry into Europe.

Policy Reforms for Faster and More Secure Processing

One challenge facing the asylum system is the long wait time for processing applications. Delays can be frustrating for genuine refugees and provide opportunities for exploitation by individuals who might misuse the system while waiting. Policy reforms that streamline the process, such as fast-track procedures for low-risk cases and specialized processing centers, help reduce the burden on asylum systems while ensuring timely protection for those in need.

1. **Fast-Track Procedures for Low-Risk Applicants**
   Some countries have introduced fast-track processing for asylum seekers from low-risk countries or those who can provide clear, verifiable evidence of their claims. By expediting cases for applicants with straightforward claims, immigration authorities can focus their resources on more complex cases, improving overall efficiency.

Example: Germany has implemented a "cluster processing" system that categorizes asylum applications based on the applicant's country of origin and likelihood of persecution. Cases from countries with high rates of approved asylum claims are prioritized, while applications from low-risk countries are processed more swiftly, allowing for faster resolution.

2. **Specialized Processing Centers and Courts**
   Specialized centers and dedicated asylum courts can help expedite the processing of applications while maintaining high standards of evaluation. These centers focus on asylum applications exclusively, enabling authorities to conduct thorough and efficient reviews. The use of dedicated asylum courts can also reduce delays in the appeals process, helping prevent prolonged detention or limbo for applicants.

Example: The United Kingdom has established specialized immigration courts to handle asylum cases, providing judges and officers with specific training in refugee law. This approach has reduced backlogs and allowed for faster decisions, especially for applicants who are detained while awaiting a decision.

3. **Transparency and Accountability in Decision-Making**

   Some countries have emphasized transparency and accountability in the asylum process to build public trust and prevent fraud. By providing clear guidelines on eligibility criteria and publishing annual reports on asylum approvals, denials, and fraud cases, governments can demonstrate the integrity of their systems and ensure that the public is informed about immigration policies.

Example: The Canadian government publishes annual reports on immigration and refugee statistics, including data on asylum applications, processing times, and fraud cases. This transparency promotes accountability and helps build public confidence in Canada's asylum system.

Reforms to Address Fraudulent Return Travel

In response to cases where refugees return to their countries of origin shortly after obtaining citizenship, several countries have implemented policies to monitor and address such behaviors. These policies seek to prevent exploitation of the asylum system by ensuring that individuals who no longer face danger in their home countries cannot continue to benefit from refugee protections.

1. **Revocation of Refugee Status and Citizenship**

   Some countries have established procedures to revoke refugee status or citizenship if an individual is found to have returned to their home country without a valid reason. This measure helps maintain the integrity of the asylum system by ensuring that individuals who no longer need protection do not continue to benefit from refugee status.

Example: In Canada, cessation hearings are used to revoke the refugee status or citizenship of individuals who have returned to their home countries. If authorities determine that a person's return indicates they no longer face danger, their refugee status may be rescinded, ensuring that protections are reserved for those genuinely at risk.

2. **Monitoring of Travel Patterns**

   Immigration authorities in some countries monitor the travel patterns of recent asylum recipients, especially in cases where return travel suggests that an individual's original claim may have been fraudulent. By tracking the travel history of new citizens or permanent residents, authorities can identify cases where individuals may have misrepresented their need for asylum.

Example: In Germany, refugees who are granted asylum are required to notify authorities if they plan to travel outside the country within a certain timeframe. Travel to the country of origin without a valid reason can trigger an investigation, potentially leading to the revocation of refugee status if fraud is suspected.

Impact of Policy Reforms on Genuine Refugees

While these reforms are necessary to prevent fraud, they can create additional challenges for genuine refugees, who may struggle to navigate increasingly complex and restrictive systems. Verification requirements, data-sharing measures, and return travel monitoring can make the asylum process feel intrusive or unwelcoming for those fleeing genuine persecution.

Balancing Security and Compassion: Genuine refugees often face obstacles in providing documentation, and the emphasis on fraud prevention may make them feel that their credibility is being questioned. It is crucial for authorities to balance the need for security with the rights of genuine asylum seekers, ensuring that the process remains accessible and respectful.

Reforms to Support Integration: To mitigate the impact of these policies on genuine refugees, some countries have implemented complementary reforms that provide support for integration. Programs such as legal assistance, trauma-informed care, and community integration services help refugees navigate the asylum process and build stable lives in their host countries.

Example: The Netherlands offers legal aid to asylum seekers, ensuring they understand the application process and their rights. This support helps genuine refugees navigate complex procedures, reducing the likelihood of misunderstandings or errors that could lead to denial.

Conclusion

Policy reforms aimed at preventing asylum fraud play a critical role in protecting the integrity of the asylum system. Enhanced verification measures, data-sharing agreements, and policies to address return travel have helped countries reduce the risk of fraud and ensure that resources are directed toward those in genuine need. However, these measures also have implications for genuine refugees, who may face increased scrutiny and additional administrative burdens.

Striking a balance between security and compassion is essential for a fair and effective asylum system. While preventing fraud is a legitimate priority, it must be done in a way that respects the dignity and rights of individuals who depend on the system for protection. Moving forward, the challenge for policymakers will be to maintain the integrity of the asylum process while ensuring that it remains accessible and just for those in true need.

Part II: Infiltration through Legal and Irregular Immigration Channels

Chapter Six: Overview of Legal Immigration Pathways

This chapter examines how legal immigration systems, which are intended to support orderly and beneficial migration, can also be exploited. It provides an overview of various legal immigration programs and highlights the vulnerabilities that can be targeted by malicious actors, posing potential security concerns for host countries.

Introduction

Legal immigration pathways are essential components of global migration systems, designed to allow individuals to enter a country based on their skills, investments, family ties, or humanitarian need. These programs serve the dual purpose of supporting national interests, such as economic growth and family unification, and providing individuals with legitimate avenues to build new lives in host countries. However, like any system, legal immigration pathways are not immune to exploitation.

This chapter examines the various types of legal immigration programs in place worldwide, including skilled worker visas, family reunification policies, investor programs, and humanitarian pathways. We will discuss how these programs are structured and consider the vulnerabilities that may be leveraged by individuals or groups with malicious intent, setting the stage for a deeper exploration of infiltration risks and misuse in later chapters.

Types of Legal Immigration Pathways

Legal immigration pathways can be broadly categorized into four main types: employment-based, family-based, investment-based, and humanitarian. Each pathway has its unique criteria, benefits, and challenges, reflecting the different priorities and goals of host countries.

1. **Employment-Based Immigration**
   Employment-based immigration allows individuals to enter a country based on their skills, qualifications, and potential contributions to the labor market. Many countries, particularly those with advanced economies, rely on skilled immigrants to fill critical gaps in sectors such as technology, healthcare, engineering, and education. Employment-based visas often require sponsorship from a local employer, who must demonstrate that the position cannot be filled by a citizen or permanent resident.

   Example: The H-1B visa in the United States allows skilled foreign professionals to work in specialized fields, such as IT, engineering, and healthcare, for a temporary period. This program has become a primary means of securing skilled foreign labor, especially from countries with strong technical education systems, like India and China. In Canada, the Global Talent Stream is a fast-track program for employers seeking highly skilled international workers, with a focus on technology and innovation sectors.

2. **Family-Based Immigration**

   Family-based immigration facilitates the reunification of families by allowing citizens and permanent residents to sponsor close relatives for residency in the host country. Family reunification policies vary by country but generally allow the sponsorship of spouses, children, parents, and sometimes siblings. This pathway is grounded in the belief that stable family units contribute positively to community and economic development.

   Example: In Canada, the Family Sponsorship Program allows Canadian citizens and permanent residents to sponsor their spouses, dependent children, parents, and grandparents for permanent residency. In the European Union, family reunification policies enable EU citizens and legal residents to bring family members to join them, as part of the EU's commitment to social cohesion.

3. **Investment-Based Immigration**

   Investment-based immigration offers residency or citizenship to individuals who make significant financial contributions to the host country's economy. These programs are often aimed at attracting wealthy individuals who can invest in local businesses, real estate, or government bonds, with the goal of stimulating economic growth and job creation. While these programs can bring substantial economic benefits, they are also susceptible to misuse, as individuals or organizations may exploit them for financial gain or strategic positioning within a foreign country.

Example: The United Kingdom's Tier 1 (Investor) Visa requires a minimum investment of £2 million in the UK economy, while Portugal's Golden Visa program grants residency to individuals who invest in real estate or create jobs. The now-defunct Canadian Immigrant Investor Program required applicants to invest CAD $800,000, which would be refunded after five years, attracting individuals with significant assets.

4. **Humanitarian Pathways**

   Humanitarian immigration pathways are established to protect individuals fleeing persecution, conflict, or environmental disasters. These pathways include refugee resettlement programs, asylum, and temporary protected status (TPS) for individuals from countries facing severe crises. Humanitarian immigration reflects a commitment to global human rights and often involves collaboration with international organizations like the United Nations High Commissioner for Refugees (UNHCR).

   Example: The United States has a robust refugee resettlement program that collaborates with UNHCR to identify and process refugees from around the world. Similarly, Germany's humanitarian visa program provides temporary protection to individuals from conflict zones or those facing persecution, with the possibility of applying for permanent residency in certain cases.

Benefits and Goals of Legal Immigration Pathways

Legal immigration pathways are designed to benefit host countries, migrants, and the global community. They fulfill several essential functions, including:

- **Economic Growth**: Skilled and investment-based immigration programs contribute to economic development by filling labor gaps, enhancing productivity, and creating jobs through investment.
- **Social Stability and Family Cohesion**: Family-based immigration supports social stability by fostering family reunification, which is critical for the mental and emotional well-being of individuals and contributes to community cohesion.
- **Humanitarian Responsibility**: Humanitarian pathways uphold the global commitment to human rights and protection, offering sanctuary to those facing persecution and violence.
- **Innovation and Knowledge Transfer**: Skilled immigrants bring new ideas, specialized knowledge, and valuable networks, fostering innovation and contributing to the global exchange of ideas.

Despite these benefits, legal immigration pathways can be exploited by individuals or groups with malicious motives, posing risks to national security and social stability.

Vulnerabilities in Legal Immigration Pathways

While legal immigration pathways are beneficial, they also present certain vulnerabilities that can be exploited. These weaknesses vary by pathway, but common themes include insufficient vetting, lack of coordination between agencies, and opportunities for manipulation by those with significant resources or sophisticated networks.

1. **Employment-Based Immigration and Skill-Based Fraud**

   Employment-based immigration pathways are susceptible to fraudulent activities such as forged credentials, fabricated work experience, and misrepresentation of skills. In some cases, individuals may use false qualifications to enter a host country under the guise of skilled labor. This can be particularly challenging to detect if verification processes are limited.

   Example: In the United States, the H-1B visa program has faced instances where applicants submitted fake degrees or falsified work experience. Employers seeking to bring foreign talent may also exaggerate job requirements to ensure approval, creating vulnerabilities in the system that can be exploited.

2. **Family-Based Immigration and Misrepresentation of Relationships**

   Family reunification policies rely heavily on documentation to verify relationships, which can be challenging to authenticate, especially in countries with limited record-keeping. Individuals may exploit family-based immigration by falsely claiming familial relationships or using fraudulent documents to establish ties with residents in the host country.

Example: Canada has encountered cases where individuals fraudulently claimed spousal relationships to gain entry through the Family Sponsorship Program. Some countries have responded by introducing DNA testing and additional vetting for family-based applications, though this raises privacy concerns and logistical challenges.

3. **Investment-Based Immigration and Financial Laundering**

Investment-based immigration is attractive to high-net-worth individuals, but it also presents an opportunity for money laundering and other forms of financial crime. Some individuals may use these programs to move money across borders under the pretext of investment, potentially "cleaning" funds derived from illicit activities. Additionally, individuals with significant financial resources may leverage investment programs to establish residency in strategic locations, potentially posing security risks.

Example: Canada's now-defunct Immigrant Investor Program attracted individuals from high-risk regions who could make the required investment or pay the interest on the investment, which effectively "cleaned" their money. Similar concerns have been raised regarding other investment programs, including Portugal's Golden Visa, which has faced scrutiny for the potential use of real estate transactions for money laundering.

4. **Humanitarian Pathways and Identity Manipulation**
   Humanitarian pathways, including refugee resettlement and asylum, are particularly vulnerable to identity manipulation due to the limited documentation available to many applicants fleeing conflict. Some individuals may exploit these pathways by assuming false identities, fabricating persecution stories, or exaggerating their need for protection. While humanitarian programs are necessary for protecting the vulnerable, they are challenging to monitor effectively.

   Example: In the EU, cases have arisen where individuals presented themselves as Syrian refugees during the height of the Syrian civil war, despite being from other regions. This misuse of humanitarian pathways has prompted European countries to implement more rigorous identity checks and verification processes.

Implications of Exploitation for Host Countries

The exploitation of legal immigration pathways can have far-reaching consequences for host countries. These implications range from security risks to social tensions and economic consequences, ultimately impacting the credibility of immigration systems.

1. **National Security Risks**

    Individuals or organizations seeking to infiltrate host countries may use legal immigration pathways to establish a foothold. For instance, agents of foreign governments or members of criminal organizations may enter under the guise of investors or skilled workers, allowing them to operate within the host country with ease. This infiltration poses significant national security risks, particularly if these individuals use their status to gather intelligence, influence public opinion, or facilitate criminal activities.

2. **Economic and Social Costs**

    Fraudulent use of immigration pathways imposes economic costs on host countries, as it requires additional resources for verification, law enforcement, and processing of applications. Additionally, misuse of these pathways can contribute to social tensions, as public opinion may turn against immigration programs, leading to calls for more restrictive policies. This skepticism can impact genuine immigrants, creating an environment of mistrust and hostility.

3. **Strain on Genuine Applicants**

    As cases of exploitation come to light, immigration authorities often respond with stricter policies and increased scrutiny, which can place additional burdens on genuine applicants. For example, heightened requirements for document verification, extensive interviews, and delays in processing can make it more challenging for legitimate immigrants to obtain residency. The result is an immigration system that becomes increasingly difficult for those who need it most.

Conclusion

Legal immigration pathways play a vital role in fostering economic growth, family unification, and humanitarian protection, but they are not without vulnerabilities. Employment-based, family-based, investment-based, and humanitarian immigration programs each present unique opportunities for exploitation, which can be used by individuals and groups with malicious intent.

As we move forward in this book, we will examine specific instances where these vulnerabilities have been exploited, including cases of foreign agents entering through investment programs, identity fraud in family reunification, and manipulation of humanitarian pathways. Understanding these risks is essential for creating policies that safeguard both the integrity of the immigration system and the security of host countries.

Chapter Seven: Agents of Malicious Organizations: Motivations and Goals

This chapter will delve into the reasons why agents of foreign governments, terrorist organizations, or criminal networks may seek to infiltrate Western countries through legal immigration pathways. This chapter will discuss the goals these individuals or groups hope to achieve, including intelligence gathering, influence operations, and financial manipulation. The chapter will also explore real-world examples that illustrate these risks.

Introduction

In a globalized world, the lines between legitimate immigration and infiltration by malicious agents can sometimes blur. Nations and organizations with adversarial interests may see immigration pathways as an opportunity to establish footholds within Western countries. Agents of foreign governments, terrorist organizations, or criminal networks may enter under the guise of legitimate immigration—be it through investment visas, skilled worker programs, or family reunification.

The motivations behind these infiltrations are varied, ranging from intelligence gathering to exerting political influence and establishing financial networks. This chapter explores these motivations and the strategies that such agents use to blend into host societies, presenting unique challenges to immigration systems and national security. We will also examine real-life examples to understand the potential consequences of infiltration by malicious actors.

Motivations for Infiltration by Malicious Agents

The primary motivations for agents of malicious organizations to enter Western countries are rooted in strategic and operational goals that align with their parent organizations. These motivations generally fall into four main categories: intelligence gathering, influence operations, financial gains, and operational freedom.

1. **Intelligence Gathering**

   One of the most common motivations for infiltrating foreign countries is intelligence gathering. Foreign governments, particularly those with adversarial relationships with Western nations, often seek information on military capabilities, technology, political strategy, and economic policies. Agents posing as legal immigrants can use their positions to access valuable information, establish networks within government and business circles, and report back to their home countries.

Example: China has been reported to use legal immigration channels to place agents in foreign universities and research institutions, where they can access sensitive research and technologies. The U.S. Federal Bureau of Investigation (FBI) has warned that certain student and research visas may be exploited by individuals gathering intelligence on behalf of the Chinese government.

2. **Influence Operations**

   Influence operations aim to manipulate public opinion, sway political decisions, or create social unrest. Agents involved in influence operations may establish connections with local communities, advocacy groups, or political organizations. By leveraging these networks, they can subtly promote narratives favorable to their home countries and influence public opinion on key issues. In some cases, influence operations are part of a larger strategy to weaken Western institutions from within by eroding trust in democratic processes.

Example: In recent years, Russia has been accused of using immigrants with connections to Russian intelligence to influence elections in Western countries. Through social media manipulation, direct funding, and relationships with community organizations, these agents promote narratives that serve Russian interests, aiming to influence public opinion and elections.

3. **Financial Manipulation and Money Laundering**

   Some agents seek to infiltrate Western countries to establish financial networks that support illicit activities, such as money laundering or fund transfers to organizations with terrorist affiliations. By gaining access to the financial systems of Western countries, they can "clean" money earned through illegal activities or channel funds to support foreign operations. Investment-based immigration programs and certain business visas are particularly susceptible to this type of exploitation, as they allow for large sums of money to enter the host country's economy with minimal oversight.

Example: Iran's Islamic Revolutionary Guard Corps (IRGC) has reportedly used legal immigration pathways, such as investment programs, to establish business fronts in Western countries. These businesses can serve as conduits for laundering money or raising funds for covert operations. By appearing legitimate, these operations can bypass regulatory scrutiny and operate within the Western financial system undetected.

4. **Operational Freedom and Strategic Positioning**

   For terrorist organizations and criminal networks, having agents embedded in Western countries provides a level of operational freedom that is difficult to achieve through other means. Once inside, these individuals can establish sleeper cells, scout potential targets, and recruit local sympathizers. Legal residency or citizenship grants them access to travel, communications, and financial systems that they might otherwise struggle to access from abroad.

Example: Hezbollah, the Lebanon-based militant group, has established networks in Western countries, including Canada and the United States, through individuals with legal status. These networks are believed to be involved in fundraising and logistical support, providing a base from which the organization could operate should it need to mobilize abroad.

Common Strategies Used by Malicious Agents

Malicious agents often adopt specific strategies to infiltrate Western nations successfully. These strategies help them maintain low profiles, establish networks, and avoid detection by immigration and security authorities.

1. **Use of Front Organizations and Shell Companies**

   Creating legitimate-looking businesses or charities allows agents to blend into society while carrying out covert activities. By establishing a front organization, agents can gain local credibility, establish relationships with key stakeholders, and conduct business operations that support their parent organizations. These companies may also serve as cover for other activities, such as recruiting locals or hosting events that promote the interests of the agent's home country.

Example: Reports have indicated that Iranian and Russian agents have used front companies in Europe to conduct influence operations, including sponsoring events that promote pro-Iranian or pro-Russian perspectives. These front organizations serve as a facade, allowing agents to build networks and gain influence without drawing direct suspicion.

2. **Networking within Key Industries**

   By entering sectors such as academia, technology, or government, malicious agents can position themselves to gain access to valuable information and relationships. This strategy is especially common in cases where agents use skilled worker or student visas, which enable them to enter highly specialized fields. Once embedded, these individuals can work toward objectives such as espionage, technology theft, or influence operations.

Example: Iranian agents have reportedly used student visas to gain entry into universities across Europe and North America, where they study nuclear engineering and other advanced sciences. This strategy allows them to acquire specialized knowledge and gather intelligence that could be leveraged to advance Iran's nuclear capabilities, raising concerns about the potential for sensitive technology transfer and the risk of misuse upon their return to Iran.

Assimilation into Local Communities and Advocacy Groups
In order to influence public opinion, some agents join local communities or advocacy groups, using these platforms to promote narratives that align with their home country's interests. This strategy is common in influence operations, where agents aim to gain the trust of locals and act as "thought leaders" within communities. By assimilating into local networks, agents can avoid suspicion and create a base of support for future operations.

Example: Russian agents have been known to integrate into cultural and religious communities in Western Europe, using their positions to promote pro-Russian narratives. These individuals may host events, publish articles, or become involved in local politics, gradually building a presence that aligns with Russian foreign policy objectives.

3. **Exploitation of Loopholes in Investment Programs**
   Investment-based immigration programs, especially those with minimal oversight, are prime targets for infiltration. By entering through investment channels, agents can establish themselves as entrepreneurs or investors, presenting themselves as individuals interested in economic opportunities. These programs are especially attractive for high-net-worth individuals with affiliations to foreign governments or terrorist organizations.

Example: Canadian intelligence agencies have raised concerns over individuals linked to foreign governments using investment programs to secure permanent residency. These individuals often invest in businesses that appear legitimate but are used to funnel funds or establish a presence for influence operations.

Real-Life Examples of Infiltration by Malicious Agents

The presence of malicious agents within Western countries is not a hypothetical concern. Various cases illustrate how these individuals have used legal immigration pathways to infiltrate countries, carry out influence operations, and even engage in espionage.

1. **Operation Ghost Stories: Russian Espionage in the United States**
   In one of the most high-profile cases of infiltration, Russian agents lived in the United States for years as part of a sleeper cell. The agents entered the country using legal pathways, blending into American society by adopting false identities, building families, and integrating into communities. Known as "Operation Ghost Stories," this espionage ring was ultimately uncovered in 2010, with the individuals involved arrested for espionage. Their goal was to gather intelligence on U.S. policies, military capabilities, and foreign relations.

2. **Iranian Influence Operations in Canada**
   Canada has documented cases of individuals with ties to Iran's IRGC using legal immigration pathways to establish businesses and organizations. These entities operate as legitimate enterprises on the surface but serve as channels for laundering funds, conducting surveillance

on Iranian dissidents, and promoting narratives favorable to the Iranian regime. Canada's immigration authorities have struggled to identify such individuals due to the sophisticated methods they use to conceal their affiliations.

3. **Chinese Influence in Australian Universities**
   Australia has faced growing concerns over Chinese influence within its educational institutions, where students and researchers affiliated with the Chinese Communist Party (CCP) have used their access to gather information on research, monitor Chinese nationals studying abroad, and promote pro-China narratives. This influence has extended to campus organizations, where agents have sought to control Chinese student associations to prevent criticism of the CCP.

Challenges in Detecting and Preventing Infiltration

The methods used by malicious agents to exploit legal immigration pathways present significant challenges for immigration and security agencies. Identifying individuals with covert intentions requires a combination of intelligence gathering, inter-agency cooperation, and advanced vetting procedures—resources that are not always readily available.

1. **Balancing Security and Privacy**
   Immigration agencies must balance the need for thorough vetting with respect for individuals' privacy rights. Measures such as social media monitoring, extensive background checks, and interviews can help identify potential risks, but they also raise concerns about personal privacy. Striking a balance between these

priorities is crucial to maintaining public support for immigration programs.

2. **Difficulty in Verifying Background Information**

   Many malicious agents enter host countries with fabricated identities or limited documentation. Verifying backgrounds is especially difficult in cases where applicants come from countries with limited record-keeping infrastructure, weak institutions, or government regimes that may obstruct efforts to confirm an individual's identity.

3. **Inconsistent International Cooperation**

   Preventing infiltration requires strong international cooperation, as intelligence about potential threats often needs to be shared between countries. However, varying policies, limited resources, and complex diplomatic relationships can hinder this cooperation, making it easier for malicious agents to slip through the cracks.

Conclusion

The infiltration of Western countries by agents of malicious organizations poses a unique and significant threat. These individuals leverage legal immigration pathways to gain entry, blending into societies while pursuing strategic objectives on behalf of foreign governments, terrorist organizations, or criminal networks. Their motivations range from intelligence gathering to influence operations, money laundering, and operational freedom, each posing unique challenges to host nations.

As we continue in Part II of this book, we will explore specific vulnerabilities within legal immigration programs that can be exploited by such agents, as well as policy measures that can be taken to safeguard national security without compromising the humanitarian mission of immigration systems.

Part II A: Subsection: Exploitation of Visa Programs

Chapter Eight: Investment-Based Infiltration

This chapter includes a hypothetical example of hostile organizations potentially investing significant sums for large-scale infiltration. This addition deepens the discussion on the risks and broader security implications of investment-based immigration programs.

Introduction

Investment-based immigration programs were initially developed to attract affluent individuals who could contribute to economic growth through substantial financial investments. These programs offer pathways to residency or citizenship for high-net-worth individuals, typically through real estate purchases, business investments, or government bonds. However, while these programs can yield economic benefits, they also create avenues for exploitation. Due to limited oversight and the large financial sums involved, investment-based immigration programs can be used not only for legitimate residency but also for money laundering, tax evasion, and even strategic infiltration by hostile foreign agents.

In this chapter, we will explore how investment-based immigration programs—particularly Canada's former Immigrant Investor Program (IIP)—have been susceptible to misuse. We'll examine how these programs can be leveraged to "clean" funds, create opportunities for intelligence operations, and enable entry for individuals who may pose national security threats. We'll also explore the broader implications of large-scale infiltration and discuss potential policy reforms to protect these systems from exploitation.

The Structure of Investment-Based Immigration Programs

Investment-based immigration programs share a common structure, although specific requirements and processes vary by country. Most programs include several core components:

1. **Minimum Investment Threshold**: Applicants must invest a minimum amount, usually in real estate, government bonds, or local businesses. This amount is often held for a fixed period, such as four to five years, after which it may be returned to the investor.
2. **Option to Pay Interest Only**: Some programs offer an option to pay the interest that the host country would gain from holding the investment rather than requiring the full investment amount upfront. This makes the program accessible to those who may not have liquid funds but can make a smaller, non-refundable payment.
3. **Pathway to Permanent Residency or Citizenship**: In return for their investment, applicants are typically

granted permanent residency, which often includes the right to bring family members. After meeting residency requirements, applicants may apply for citizenship, giving them full legal rights in the host country.

4. **Limited Security Vetting**: While financial eligibility is verified, many investment-based immigration programs do not apply rigorous security checks. This lack of vetting can allow individuals or organizations with malicious intent to enter under the guise of investors.

Example: Canada's Immigrant Investor Program (IIP) required applicants to invest CAD $800,000 for five years. Alternatively, they could pay approximately CAD $200,000 in non-refundable interest, bypassing the need to deposit the full amount. Successful applicants were granted permanent residency and a path to Canadian citizenship, allowing them and their families to settle in Canada and eventually apply for Canadian passports.

Motivations for Exploitation by Hostile Entities

Investment-based immigration programs are particularly attractive to foreign agents, criminal networks, and even terrorist organizations. These actors are motivated by several strategic goals that align well with the benefits offered by these immigration programs.

1. **Access to Residency and Citizenship**
   For agents of hostile states or organizations, residency and citizenship in a Western country provide access to key infrastructure, legal protections, and freedoms. These individuals can operate under the cover of legitimacy, moving freely within the host country and

internationally. Citizenship also enables them to establish bases of operation in allied countries, making it easier to gather intelligence or coordinate influence operations.

2. **Opportunity for Money Laundering**
Investment-based immigration programs are attractive to individuals looking to launder funds derived from criminal or illicit activities. By "investing" in real estate or businesses, these funds are essentially "cleaned" and legitimized by the host country's system. Once withdrawn, these funds appear to be legitimate earnings, free of their original criminal associations.

3. **Strategic Positioning for Intelligence Operations**
By embedding agents in key regions, hostile organizations can conduct surveillance, gather intelligence, and cultivate networks without attracting suspicion. Residency or citizenship gained through investment programs allows these agents to work within Western nations and establish long-term strategic positions.

4. **Large-Scale Infiltration for Potential Covert Operations**
For organizations with considerable financial resources, such as certain states or powerful criminal networks, investment-based immigration provides a pathway for large-scale infiltration. Imagine a regime or terrorist organization investing one billion dollars into such a project. This sum could secure hundreds or even thousands of residency or citizenship approvals. For example, with the option to pay interest instead of the full investment amount, agents could potentially enter a country like Canada at a relatively low cost. Once

established, these agents would have access to Canadian passports, which enable visa-free or visa-on-arrival travel to numerous Western countries, including the United States and much of Europe.

Implications: This scenario highlights the scale of infiltration that could be achieved if a hostile organization used investment-based immigration strategically. With hundreds of agents positioned within a target country, they could conduct coordinated influence operations, gather intelligence, and create sleeper cells with minimal detection risk. For Western nations, such large-scale infiltration poses serious security concerns, as it could undermine intelligence operations, disrupt critical infrastructure, or erode public trust in institutions.

Case Study: Canada's Immigrant Investor Program (IIP)

Canada's IIP, active from 1986 until its termination in 2014, illustrates both the potential benefits and significant risks of investment-based immigration programs. Designed to attract wealthy investors, the program required applicants to make a substantial financial commitment to Canada's economy. Applicants could choose to pay only the interest on this amount, effectively bypassing the need for a full upfront investment.

1. **Residency and Citizenship Pathway**
   The IIP offered applicants a fast track to permanent residency and, after fulfilling residency requirements, Canadian citizenship. For individuals and families from regions of geopolitical instability or restricted mobility, the IIP provided a legal and relatively quick path to a Canadian passport. This access was particularly valuable

for those seeking to avoid the scrutiny that individuals from high-risk regions often face when applying for visas or residency in Western countries.

2. **Potential for Money Laundering**

   One of the program's most significant vulnerabilities was its capacity for money laundering. High-net-worth individuals could move large sums of money into Canada under the guise of investment, which was returned to them at the end of the term. This "investment" effectively allowed for funds of potentially illicit origin to be legitimized by the Canadian financial system, facilitating access to clean, transferable funds that could be used internationally.

3. **Exploitation by Agents of Hostile Organizations**

   The limited vetting procedures in place for the IIP left it vulnerable to exploitation by individuals with connections to hostile organizations. Reports indicate that individuals associated with Iran's Islamic Revolutionary Guard Corps (IRGC) and other high-risk entities used the IIP to secure Canadian residency. With a Canadian passport, these individuals could easily travel to and operate in the United States, the European Union, and other allied nations.

Implications for North American Security:

Canadian intelligence agencies raised concerns that such infiltration could pose threats not only to Canada but to the United States as well, given the ease with which Canadian citizens can travel to the U.S. If agents associated with hostile regimes gained residency or citizenship through the IIP, they could potentially use Canada as a strategic base for operations in North America.

Examples from Other Countries

Canada's IIP is not the only program that has faced criticism for its potential security risks. Similar vulnerabilities have been identified in other investment-based immigration programs worldwide.

1. **Portugal's Golden Visa Program**
   Portugal's Golden Visa program, which offers residency in exchange for investments in real estate or job creation, has attracted considerable foreign investment. However, it has also raised concerns about money laundering, as real estate transactions tied to the program provide a convenient way to "clean" funds. Critics argue that the program has limited oversight, making it vulnerable to exploitation by individuals looking to launder large sums of money.

2. **Cyprus Investment Program**
   Cyprus's citizenship-by-investment program, which offered Cypriot passports in exchange for investments in property or government bonds, was terminated in 2020 after it was discovered that individuals with criminal backgrounds and ties to hostile organizations had obtained citizenship. Cypriot passports grant access to the European Union, allowing these individuals to travel freely throughout the EU and establish business fronts with minimal scrutiny.

3. **The United Kingdom's Tier 1 (Investor) Visa**
   The UK's Tier 1 (Investor) visa required applicants to

invest a minimum of £2 million in UK assets. Reports indicated that the visa attracted high-net-worth individuals from Russia, China, and the Middle East, some of whom were linked to state-affiliated intelligence agencies or criminal networks. These individuals could establish business interests in the UK and access sensitive industries, raising concerns about their potential for influence or manipulation.

Risks and Implications for Host Countries

The vulnerabilities associated with investment-based immigration programs have significant implications for host countries, affecting national security, economic stability, and international relations.

1. **Infiltration by Foreign Intelligence Agents**
   Foreign agents who gain residency or citizenship through investment programs are positioned to conduct intelligence-gathering operations with minimal risk of exposure. With access to legal residency, these agents can establish relationships, infiltrate institutions, and gather intelligence on political, economic, and technological developments.

2. **Money Laundering and Economic Distortion**
   Investment programs provide ample opportunities for money laundering, enabling individuals to move illicit funds into legitimate investments. The influx of foreign capital, especially into real estate, can distort local economies by driving up property prices and reducing affordability for residents.

3. **Impact on Allied Nations**

   Countries with lax investment-based immigration policies can inadvertently undermine the security of their allies. For example, individuals with Canadian residency or citizenship can travel freely to the United States, which raises security concerns for the U.S. Similarly, EU member states that offer investment-based citizenship may inadvertently compromise the security of the entire Schengen Area.

Measures to Mitigate Exploitation

To prevent exploitation, several countries have introduced reforms to strengthen the integrity of their investment-based immigration programs. These measures include enhanced vetting, financial transparency, and data-sharing among allied nations.

1. **Stricter Background Checks and Financial Audits**

   More rigorous background checks are essential to identify high-risk individuals. Countries are increasingly requiring applicants to provide evidence of the origins of their funds, and financial audits are conducted to verify the legitimacy of the investment capital.

2. **Transparency in Real Estate Transactions**

   To reduce money laundering in real estate, some countries require that property purchases associated with investment visas be fully transparent. This includes public registries of property owners and mandatory reporting of foreign investment transactions.

3. **Data Sharing and International Cooperation**

   Collaborating with international partners is crucial for

identifying individuals who may pose security risks. Data-sharing agreements between allied countries enable cross-referencing of applicant information with watchlists and intelligence reports, providing a more comprehensive assessment of risk.

Conclusion

Investment-based immigration programs, while economically beneficial, are vulnerable to exploitation by hostile actors and criminal organizations. By examining Canada's Immigrant Investor Program and similar initiatives globally, we see the serious risks these programs pose, including potential infiltration by agents of hostile regimes, large-scale money laundering, and threats to national and allied security.

To protect these programs from abuse, policymakers must balance the economic incentives of investment-based immigration with robust security measures. This includes more stringent background checks, enhanced transparency in investments, and international cooperation to prevent malicious actors from leveraging these programs for covert operations. The next chapter will delve into further vulnerabilities in immigration pathways, exploring how family-based programs can also be manipulated for infiltration and security risks.

Chapter Nine: Exploiting Family Reunification Programs for Infiltration

This chapter explores the vulnerabilities of family reunification programs, including examples of potential misuse involving fraudulent relationships, such as attempts to bring second wives or other family members under false pretenses. It provides a comprehensive overview of the risks and challenges faced by these programs, highlighting how they can be exploited by individuals with malicious intent.

Introduction

Family reunification is a foundational principle in many immigration systems, allowing individuals to bring close family members to join them in their new country. These programs are intended to support social cohesion by strengthening family units, which play a critical role in the well-being and integration of immigrants. However, family reunification programs can also be exploited, providing avenues for individuals to enter under false pretenses or gain legal residency through fabricated familial connections.

This chapter explores the structure of family reunification programs, the vulnerabilities within these systems, and how they are susceptible to manipulation. By examining cases from Canada, the United States, and Europe, we'll uncover examples of fraud and misrepresentation, such as individuals claiming false family ties or sponsors bringing second wives or family members under misleading roles like domestic workers. These cases highlight the need for robust verification procedures to prevent exploitation while ensuring that genuine applicants receive the support they deserve.

Structure and Purpose of Family Reunification Programs

Family reunification policies are designed to allow immigrants and citizens to reunite with close family members, fostering emotional and social stability. These policies generally support the sponsorship of immediate family members, including spouses, children, and, in some cases, parents or siblings. The goal is to strengthen communities by allowing family units to remain intact, thus supporting the well-being of immigrants and encouraging successful integration.

1. **Eligibility Requirements and Sponsorship Obligations**
   Family reunification programs require that sponsors demonstrate their legal status, usually as citizens or permanent residents, along with proof of their relationship to the applicant. Sponsors are often subject to financial criteria to ensure they can support their relatives without reliance on public assistance. Documentation such as marriage certificates, birth records, or adoption papers is typically required to verify relationships.
2. **Residency Pathway for Family Members**
   Approved applicants under family reunification programs receive residency status, with the possibility of

pursuing citizenship after fulfilling residency requirements. This pathway provides stability, allowing family members to access healthcare, education, and employment opportunities in the host country, ultimately benefiting the broader community by encouraging family cohesion.

3. **Limited Verification of Relationship Authenticity**
   Family reunification programs prioritize relationship verification but often lack rigorous security checks. While basic documentation is required, comprehensive checks of relationship authenticity can be challenging, particularly in cases where applicants originate from countries with limited record-keeping. This limited vetting process opens the door to exploitation, allowing individuals to potentially fabricate family connections or bypass restrictions on polygamy and other practices not recognized in Western legal systems.

Example: Canada's Family Sponsorship Program allows Canadian citizens and permanent residents to sponsor their spouses, dependent children, parents, and grandparents. While the program plays a crucial role in family unity, it has occasionally been exploited through misrepresentation or fraudulent documentation.

Exploitation Tactics and Vulnerabilities

The structure of family reunification programs presents specific vulnerabilities that can be exploited by individuals or groups with fraudulent intentions. These vulnerabilities include false claims of familial relationships, documentation forgery, and misrepresentation of the true nature of relationships. Here are some of the common tactics used to exploit family reunification programs:

1. **False Claims of Marital or Familial Relationships**
   A significant vulnerability in family reunification programs lies in the potential for applicants to misrepresent relationships. Some individuals may falsely claim to be a spouse, child, or sibling of a sponsor to gain entry to the host country. This tactic is challenging to detect, especially for applicants from regions with weak or inconsistent record-keeping, where verifying the authenticity of relationships is difficult.

Example: In the United States, authorities have encountered cases where individuals claimed false marriages to U.S. citizens to obtain residency. Some of these relationships were arranged specifically to secure immigration benefits, with parties paying "marriage brokers" to help facilitate these arrangements. These marriages are often quickly dissolved once residency is achieved, revealing the transactional nature of the arrangement.

2. **Bringing Second Wives under False Titles**
   In some cases, individuals from countries where polygamy is culturally accepted, such as Afghanistan or certain regions of the Middle East, have attempted to bring a second wife into Western countries where polygamy is not legally recognized. To circumvent restrictions, the second wife is sometimes brought in under the pretense of being a domestic worker, nanny, or caregiver. This tactic exploits the limited scrutiny applied to domestic worker visas and family reunification

applications, allowing individuals to bypass legal restrictions on polygamous relationships.

Example: In Canada, immigration authorities have occasionally uncovered cases where individuals attempted to bring second wives into the country as nannies or household staff. These arrangements are presented as employment-based immigration, but in reality, the relationship between the applicant and sponsor is marital. Detecting such cases can be challenging, as the individuals may present forged employment contracts or manipulate their personal history to avoid suspicion. Although these cases are rare and often go unreported, they illustrate the potential for family reunification programs to be misused in ways that violate Western legal norms.

3. **Documentation Fraud and Identity Manipulation**
   Document fraud is a common tactic in family reunification programs. Applicants may submit forged birth certificates, marriage certificates, or adoption papers to establish a familial link to the sponsor. In regions with limited infrastructure, such as conflict-affected areas, it is particularly challenging for immigration authorities to verify documents, making it easier for individuals to create false identities or misrepresent familial relationships.

Example: In Canada, authorities have encountered instances where applicants from conflict regions submitted fraudulent documents to establish family ties. In one case, an individual claimed that a woman was his spouse, submitting a marriage certificate from his home country. However, it was later revealed that the document was forged, and the relationship was fabricated to facilitate her entry. Without access to reliable records, detecting such fraud often relies on in-depth investigations that are resource-intensive.

4. **Misrepresentation of Dependency Status**

   Some family reunification applications involve applicants who falsely claim dependency to qualify for sponsorship. This is particularly common in cases where adults pose as dependent children or elderly parents misrepresent their financial or physical reliance on the sponsor. These misrepresentations can go undetected if authorities lack the resources or evidence to verify the true nature of the dependency.

Example: In European countries, including Germany and the United Kingdom, immigration officials have identified cases where adult individuals claimed to be the dependent children of sponsors. These applicants provided altered birth certificates and other documents to create the appearance of dependency. In some cases, sponsors misrepresented elderly family members as dependents, even though they were financially independent, to bring them into the country under more lenient family reunification policies.

Challenges in Detection and Prevention

Detecting and preventing exploitation in family reunification programs is a complex task for immigration authorities. The clandestine nature of some of these tactics, combined with limited resources, makes it challenging to verify all claims thoroughly. Here are some of the key challenges authorities face in managing family reunification programs:

1. **Difficulty Verifying Relationships from Conflict Zones**

    Many applicants come from countries with limited administrative infrastructure, such as Afghanistan, Syria, and Somalia. In these regions, official records may be scarce, making it difficult for immigration authorities to confirm the authenticity of documents. Additionally, some individuals may have genuine relationships that are undocumented, further complicating the process of verification.

2. **Limited Resources for Thorough Investigation**

    Comprehensive verification of family relationships requires time, resources, and specialized training, particularly when applicants come from high-risk regions. Immigration agencies often face resource constraints that limit their ability to conduct in-depth investigations on every application, leaving the door open for exploitation.

3. **Legal and Privacy Concerns in Verification Processes**

    In some countries, privacy laws limit the extent to which immigration authorities can investigate personal relationships. For example, verifying claims through intrusive questioning or mandatory DNA testing can raise ethical and privacy concerns. While these measures may be effective in detecting fraud, they also risk infringing on applicants' rights and may deter genuine applicants from pursuing reunification.

4. **Complexity of Detecting Relationship Fraud Involving Second Wives or Multiple Partners**

    In cases where individuals bring second wives under the guise of domestic workers, it can be particularly challenging to identify the true nature of the relationship. Agents may present legitimate-looking employment contracts, and the individuals involved may be coached to provide consistent accounts. Uncovering these cases often requires extensive background checks and in-depth interviews, which may not be feasible in all cases.

Policy Measures to Prevent Exploitation of Family Reunification Programs

To address the risks associated with family reunification programs, several countries have introduced policies aimed at strengthening verification processes and preventing exploitation. These measures are designed to protect the integrity of family reunification programs while ensuring that genuine applicants can still access support.

1. **Enhanced Verification of Documents**
   Some countries have invested in technologies and partnerships to improve the verification of documents from high-risk regions. For instance, digital verification systems, consular verification, and collaboration with international organizations can help confirm the authenticity of documents, reducing the likelihood of fraud.
2. **Increased Scrutiny for Domestic Worker Visas Associated with Family Sponsors**
   To prevent individuals from misrepresenting second wives as domestic workers, some countries have introduced increased scrutiny for domestic worker visas associated with family sponsorship. This includes interviews with both the sponsor and applicant, requiring

sponsors to prove the necessity of the domestic worker role, and more rigorous background checks.

3. **Mandatory DNA Testing for High-Risk Cases**

   In cases where relationships cannot be verified through documentation alone, some immigration authorities have implemented mandatory DNA testing to confirm biological relationships. While this measure raises privacy concerns, it can be highly effective in identifying fraud, particularly in cases involving minors or dependent claims. DNA testing is typically reserved for cases from regions with high rates of document fraud or known vulnerabilities in family reunification programs.

4. **Improved Training for Immigration Officers**

   Immigration officers involved in family reunification processing can benefit from specialized training in detecting signs of fraud, conducting effective interviews, and understanding cultural nuances that may indicate potential misrepresentation. Improved training equips officers with the tools to better assess relationships and identify potential cases of exploitation.

Conclusion

Family reunification programs are essential for promoting social cohesion and supporting the integration of immigrants by keeping families together. However, these programs are vulnerable to exploitation, as individuals and groups with fraudulent intentions may attempt to manipulate familial relationships or documentation to gain entry into a host country. By examining cases in Canada, the U.S., and Europe, this chapter highlights the tactics used to exploit these pathways, including false claims of dependency, misrepresentation of relationships, and the practice of bringing second wives under false pretenses.

To prevent such exploitation, immigration authorities must balance privacy rights with effective verification procedures, implementing measures such as enhanced document checks, targeted interviews, and, in some cases, DNA testing. Strengthening the integrity of family reunification programs not only protects national security but also ensures that genuine families receive the support they need to integrate and thrive in their new communities.

Chapter Ten: Employment-Based Immigration Pathways and Security Risks

This chapter explores the structure of employment-based immigration programs, their importance in addressing labor shortages and fostering economic growth, and how they can be exploited. We'll discuss vulnerabilities within these pathways, including cases where individuals misrepresent qualifications or affiliations and how some may use employment visas to infiltrate sensitive sectors. Real-world examples and recommendations for policy reforms will provide a comprehensive view of the challenges and solutions in employment-based immigration.

Introduction

Employment-based immigration pathways serve as vital tools for countries to fill labor shortages, attract skilled talent, and promote economic development. By granting visas to professionals and skilled workers, these programs enable countries to compete in a global marketplace, accessing a broader pool of talent in fields like technology, healthcare, engineering, and education. However, while these programs bring significant benefits, they are not without risks. Employment-based immigration pathways can also be exploited by individuals with fraudulent credentials or by agents working for foreign states or criminal organizations.

This chapter examines the benefits and structure of employment-based immigration programs, highlighting their role in supporting economic growth. We will also discuss the specific vulnerabilities within these pathways and how they can be exploited by malicious actors. Real-world examples from Canada, the United States, and the European Union will illustrate these risks, along with a discussion on potential policy reforms to enhance the security and integrity of employment-based immigration programs.

Structure and Purpose of Employment-Based Immigration Pathways

Employment-based immigration programs are designed to address workforce shortages by attracting skilled workers from abroad. These programs benefit both employers, who gain access to a diverse talent pool, and immigrants, who are given the opportunity to secure stable employment and potentially pursue permanent residency or citizenship in their host country. The structure of these programs varies by country, but generally includes key elements:

1. **Employer Sponsorship**
   In many employment-based immigration programs, employers must sponsor the applicant, demonstrating that the position could not be filled by a citizen or permanent resident. The employer often takes responsibility for verifying the applicant's qualifications and providing a job offer, which serves as a prerequisite for the visa application.
2. **Qualification and Skill Requirements**
   Employment-based visas are typically reserved for

individuals with specialized skills, advanced education, or experience in high-demand sectors. Applicants may be required to present academic transcripts, certifications, or references to verify their expertise. Commonly targeted fields include technology, healthcare, science, engineering, and finance.

3. **Temporary and Permanent Residency Options**
Employment-based immigration programs often offer both temporary work permits and pathways to permanent residency. Temporary visas allow individuals to work for a specific employer for a limited time, while permanent residency options enable long-term stability and, in some cases, a pathway to citizenship.

4. **Limited Security Screening and Oversight**
The primary focus of employment-based immigration programs is on verifying an applicant's skills and qualifications. Security checks are typically less comprehensive than in refugee or asylum programs, as employment-based applicants are generally assumed to be low-risk. This limited oversight can create opportunities for exploitation, as individuals with fraudulent credentials or malicious intent may use these programs to enter the host country.

Example: The United States H-1B visa program is a prominent employment-based immigration pathway that allows skilled foreign workers to fill specialized positions. Many workers in information technology, healthcare, and engineering use the H-1B program as a means to gain work experience in the U.S., with the possibility of pursuing permanent residency after a few years.

Vulnerabilities in Employment-Based Immigration Pathways

While employment-based immigration pathways offer significant economic benefits, they are vulnerable to specific forms of exploitation. The most common risks include document fraud, misrepresentation of skills, and infiltration into sensitive industries. These vulnerabilities can be exploited by individuals or groups seeking to gain entry for purposes other than legitimate employment.

1. **Credential and Documentation Fraud**

   One of the primary vulnerabilities in employment-based immigration programs is the potential for individuals to submit falsified credentials. Some applicants may present fake degrees, certifications, or references to qualify for positions in high-demand sectors. In regions where verification systems are limited, it can be difficult for immigration authorities to confirm the legitimacy of these documents.

Example: In the U.S. H-1B visa program, cases have surfaced where applicants submitted fake diplomas or employment history to qualify for skilled positions. These cases highlight the difficulty of verifying credentials from regions with limited educational oversight, where fraudulent degrees can be purchased.

2. **Misrepresentation of Job Requirements by Employers**

   Employers, particularly in technology and engineering sectors, may misrepresent job requirements to ensure approval of a visa application. This practice allows companies to bring in workers at lower costs than hiring domestic employees, circumventing regulations intended to prioritize local talent. While this tactic is often economically motivated, it can also open the door to individuals who may not meet the advertised qualifications.

Example: In Canada, reports indicate that some companies in the tech industry have misrepresented job roles to gain approval for foreign workers under the Global Talent Stream, a fast-track employment visa program. This misrepresentation complicates regulatory oversight and makes it more challenging for immigration authorities to monitor applicant qualifications accurately.

3. **Infiltration into Sensitive Industries**

   Employment-based immigration programs present an attractive opportunity for agents of foreign governments or organizations seeking access to sensitive information or technologies. By entering sectors like technology, defense, or healthcare, these individuals can gain access to proprietary research, intellectual property, or critical infrastructure. Once inside, they may act as covert operatives, conducting intelligence gathering, espionage, or cyber-operations on behalf of their parent organization.

Example: Several Western countries, including the United States and Canada, have raised concerns about foreign nationals from specific countries gaining access to sensitive industries, particularly in research and technology. These concerns have prompted increased scrutiny on foreign researchers and employees in sectors such as artificial intelligence, nuclear engineering, and biopharmaceuticals.

4. **Use of Shell Companies to Facilitate Entry**

   Another tactic used to exploit employment-based immigration pathways is the creation of shell companies. Malicious actors establish fake companies to "hire" individuals who then apply for visas through these organizations. Once granted entry, the individuals may have no real employment duties but instead operate for ulterior motives, such as establishing a base for influence operations, espionage, or other covert activities.

Example: In the European Union, immigration authorities have encountered cases where shell companies were created by individuals associated with criminal networks. These companies existed solely to facilitate visa applications, allowing foreign nationals to gain residency without legitimate employment.

Real-World Examples of Exploitation

The potential for misuse in employment-based immigration pathways is not hypothetical. Several documented cases illustrate how these pathways can be exploited for infiltration, fraud, and access to sensitive sectors. Here are some real-world examples from the United States, Canada, and the European Union.

1. **Chinese Nationals in U.S. Research Labs**

   The United States has raised concerns about foreign nationals, particularly from China, using employment-based visas to enter U.S. research institutions and access sensitive technologies. In several cases, individuals affiliated with the Chinese government were found to be gathering intelligence or copying intellectual property for use in state-run projects. The Federal Bureau of Investigation (FBI) has increased surveillance on individuals from high-risk countries entering fields like nuclear engineering, cybersecurity, and artificial intelligence.

2. **Russian Influence in European Technology Sectors**
   Europe has documented cases where foreign nationals, including Russian individuals with government affiliations, entered the technology sector using employment visas. Some of these individuals were later identified as operatives engaged in influence operations or intelligence gathering. The European Union has since increased scrutiny of applicants from high-risk countries applying for roles in technology and engineering sectors.

3. **Investment and Shell Companies in Canada**
   Canada has encountered cases of individuals using employment-based immigration programs as a pathway to establish front companies for criminal activities. In one instance, a shell company in the technology sector was created to sponsor foreign nationals who later engaged in cyber operations linked to foreign intelligence agencies. Canadian authorities now work closely with intelligence partners to identify potential threats in high-risk sectors.

Policy Measures to Mitigate Risks

To address the risks associated with employment-based immigration pathways, several countries have introduced measures to improve verification, increase transparency, and enhance security screening processes. Here are some policy recommendations and measures currently being implemented:

1. **Enhanced Credential Verification**

   Countries are adopting digital verification systems to authenticate educational and professional credentials. These systems cross-reference applicants' qualifications with university records, licensing bodies, and professional associations, reducing the likelihood of fraudulent submissions.

Example: The European Union is piloting a digital credential verification platform that allows immigration authorities to access academic records and verify degrees through a secure online portal, improving the accuracy of credential checks.

2. **Improved Employer Accountability**

   Governments have introduced stricter regulations to hold employers accountable for misrepresenting job requirements. Employers sponsoring foreign workers may be required to provide more extensive documentation, including proof of local hiring efforts and justification for hiring foreign talent. Additionally, employers may face penalties if found to have manipulated job descriptions or misrepresented roles to secure visas.

Example: In Canada's Global Talent Stream, employers are required to submit detailed applications demonstrating their efforts to hire locally before sponsoring foreign workers. The program also includes periodic audits to ensure compliance, with penalties for employers who violate program regulations.

3. **Screening for High-Risk Sectors**

   In response to concerns about infiltration in sensitive industries, some countries have introduced specialized vetting for employment-based visa applicants in high-risk fields. This screening includes more comprehensive background checks, cross-referencing with intelligence databases, and closer scrutiny of applicants from countries with known security concerns.

Example: The United States has implemented additional screening for applicants entering fields related to national security, such as cybersecurity, nuclear engineering, and biotechnology. Applicants from high-risk countries may be subject to longer processing times and additional checks to assess potential security risks.

4. **Increased Collaboration with Intelligence Agencies**

   Immigration authorities are strengthening their partnerships with national intelligence agencies to identify high-risk applicants before they gain access to sensitive sectors. By sharing intelligence on known operatives, foreign agents, and criminal associates, immigration authorities can better assess applications and prevent infiltration.

Example: Canada and the United Kingdom have enhanced data-sharing agreements with intelligence allies to monitor and track applicants from high-risk regions applying for employment-based visas. These collaborations provide additional layers of security and enable faster responses to potential threats.

5. **Audits and On-Site Inspections**
   Regular audits and on-site inspections of companies employing foreign workers help ensure that applicants are fulfilling their stated roles and that companies are compliant with immigration regulations. This measure is especially effective in detecting shell companies and verifying the legitimacy of job placements.

Example: The United States Citizenship and Immigration Services (USCIS) conducts random audits and workplace inspections for H-1B visa employers to confirm that foreign employees are performing legitimate work and that employers are adhering to program requirements.

Conclusion

Employment-based immigration pathways are critical for filling labor shortages and promoting innovation, but they also present unique security risks. From credential fraud to infiltration by foreign operatives, these programs can be exploited by individuals with malicious intentions. Real-world cases from the U.S., Canada, and Europe illustrate how employment-based visas have been used to gain entry into sensitive industries, enabling espionage, influence operations, and criminal activity.

To protect the integrity of these pathways, host countries must implement stronger verification processes, increase accountability for employers, and collaborate with intelligence agencies to monitor high-risk applicants. These measures will help prevent exploitation while ensuring that employment-based immigration continues to serve its intended purpose: supporting economic growth and innovation by attracting skilled, genuine talent from around the world.

Chapter Eleven: Exploitation of Student Visa Programs: The Case of Canada

This chapter explores the vulnerabilities within Canada's student visa programs, highlighting recent cases of visa fraud and the exploitation of international students. We will examine how fraudulent agents and smugglers exploit students using fake admission letters and false promises, leading to financial exploitation and the risk of deportation. The chapter also discusses the broader impact on Canada's immigration system and outlines policy recommendations to protect students and maintain program integrity.

Introduction

This chapter explores the vulnerabilities and abuses of student visa programs, particularly in Canada, which have recently gained international attention due to significant cases of visa fraud and the exploitation of international students. Student visa programs are designed to attract talent, foster cultural exchange, and provide educational opportunities. However, the system has become a target for both fraudulent agents and human smugglers who exploit aspiring students for financial gain. This chapter will delve into how student visas are exploited, the consequences for international students, and the broader implications for the Canadian immigration system. We will also examine recent examples and discuss the need for reforms to safeguard the integrity of the system.

The Rise of International Education and the Student Visa Program

International education has become a significant element of Canada's immigration strategy, contributing billions of dollars annually to the economy. The government has promoted Canada as an attractive destination for students due to its quality education, safe environment, and potential pathways to permanent residency. Students from around the world are drawn to Canadian institutions, seeking not only academic growth but also opportunities to establish themselves in one of the world's leading economies.

While the growth of international students has had positive effects—boosting enrollment in educational institutions, increasing diversity, and enriching academic environments—it has also exposed certain vulnerabilities. These vulnerabilities have led to cases of fraud, where students are either knowingly or unknowingly involved in schemes orchestrated by fraudulent agents These abuses have recently culminated in a high-profile scandal, highlighting the fragility of the student visa system.

Fraudulent Admission Letters and the 2023 Deportation Crisis

In 2023, a scandal involving hundreds of international students in Canada brought the exploitation of student visas to the forefront. It was discovered that many students had entered Canada using fraudulent admission letters, which they had obtained through unscrupulous agents in their home countries. These agents, often posing as legitimate immigration consultants, charged substantial fees to help students secure visas, promising admission to Canadian institutions that were either unaware of these applications or that did not exist.

The students, many of whom were unaware that their admission letters were fraudulent, arrived in Canada and began their studies or sought employment, believing their paperwork was in order. It was only years later, when these students began applying for permanent residency, that immigration officials discovered discrepancies. The fraudulent admission letters led to orders of deportation, creating a wave of fear and uncertainty among the affected students.

The Canadian government's response included temporarily halting deportations and creating a task force to individually assess each case. Public outrage and advocacy from various stakeholders, including student unions and human rights organizations, prompted the government to reconsider blanket deportations. Many argued that these students were victims of deceitful agents, and deporting them would only further victimize individuals who had invested their savings and future into pursuing education in Canada.

This case underscores the vulnerability of international students who rely on third-party agents to navigate complex immigration processes. The lack of robust verification mechanisms in some countries, combined with the high demand for student visas, has created a perfect storm for exploitation.

Human Smuggling and Financial Exploitation
Another layer of exploitation faced by international students involves human smuggling and exorbitant financial demands. In recent years, there have been cases of human smugglers advertising illegal border crossings or fake immigration pathways to Canada. These smugglers often target desperate students who have been denied legitimate visas or who are looking for alternative routes to enter the country.

The financial exploitation does not end with fake visa services. Once in Canada, some students find themselves indebted to the very agents or smugglers who facilitated their entry. This debt can lead to forced labor or other forms of exploitation, as students struggle to repay the money they borrowed for forged documents or illegal crossings. The financial strain also forces some students to work long hours—sometimes in unsafe conditions—which jeopardizes their studies and well-being.

Challenges Faced by International Students
International students who fall victim to fraudulent agents face a multitude of challenges. First, they often struggle with their legal status, as many arrive believing they have followed all necessary procedures, only to find out later that their visas are invalid. This uncertainty about their status leads to mental health struggles, fear of deportation, and a lack of stability.

Moreover, many students arrive in Canada without a clear understanding of their rights or the resources available to them. Language barriers, cultural differences, and the complexities of Canadian immigration law make it difficult for them to seek help. Fraudulent agents often take advantage of this knowledge gap, ensuring that students remain unaware of their rights or the recourse available in cases of exploitation.

Consequences for Canada's Immigration System
The exploitation of the student visa program not only affects the individuals directly involved but also has broader implications for Canada's immigration system. Cases of fraud undermine public trust in the integrity of the system and fuel anti-immigrant sentiments. When high-profile cases of visa fraud emerge, they often lead to calls for more restrictive immigration policies,

which ultimately impact genuine students and other immigrants seeking to come to Canada.

The economic impact is also significant. Canada's reputation as a welcoming destination for international students is at risk when cases of fraud and exploitation come to light. Educational institutions, which rely heavily on tuition fees from international students, may also suffer as potential applicants become wary of falling victim to fraudulent schemes. This has prompted both educational institutions and the government to take a more proactive approach in preventing fraud and protecting students.

Examples of Exploitation without Naming Individuals or Institutions

Consider a case where a student from South Asia was approached by an education agent who promised admission to a well-known college in Canada. The agent provided an official-looking admission letter and helped the student obtain a visa. The student paid thousands of dollars in fees, only to discover upon arrival that the college had no record of their admission. Left in a foreign country with an invalid visa, the student faced the risk of deportation and had no recourse to recover the money paid to the agent.

In another scenario, a group of students from Central America was promised work permits upon completion of their studies. They were charged hefty fees for these services, only to find out later that the work permits were fake. Unable to legally work and burdened with debt, these students faced precarious situations, with some being forced to take up exploitative jobs to make ends meet.

Policy Considerations and Recommendations

To address the vulnerabilities in the student visa program, several policy measures can be implemented to prevent fraud and protect international students. One of the most critical steps is enhancing the verification process for admission letters and educational institutions. The Canadian government, in collaboration with educational institutions, could establish a centralized system where visa officers can verify the legitimacy of admission offers directly with the institutions.

Public awareness campaigns are also crucial. Prospective students must be informed about the risks of using unauthorized agents and the importance of verifying the credentials of anyone offering immigration services. Governments can work with embassies and consulates to provide accurate information and resources to students before they apply for visas.

Another recommendation is to increase oversight of education agents. Many countries lack regulation of education consultants, allowing fraudulent agents to operate unchecked. By implementing a licensing system and holding agents accountable for misconduct, the government can reduce the prevalence of fraudulent practices.

There should also be stronger penalties for those found guilty of exploiting international students. This includes not only fraudulent agents but also employers who take advantage of students' vulnerable status by underpaying them or forcing them into unsafe work environments. Establishing hotlines and support services for international students can also provide them with the means to report exploitation without fear of retaliation.

Conclusion

The exploitation of student visa programs in Canada highlights the need for a more robust and transparent system that protects international students and preserves the integrity of the immigration process. Recent cases of deportation due to fraudulent admission letters, combined with ongoing issues of human smuggling and financial exploitation, underscore the vulnerabilities that exist within the current system.

By enhancing verification processes, regulating education agents, and providing better support and resources to international students, Canada can continue to be a destination of choice for those seeking quality education. The challenge lies in balancing the need for growth in international education with the responsibility to protect those who come seeking a better future. By addressing these challenges head-on, Canada can ensure that its student visa program remains a pathway to opportunity rather than exploitation.

Part II B: Subsection: Exploitation of Visa Programs

Chapter Twelve: Exploitation of LGBTQ Protections in the Asylum System

This chapter examines how LGBTQ protections in asylum systems, intended to protect individuals fleeing persecution, are sometimes exploited by those seeking to manipulate the process. We explore the challenges immigration authorities face in assessing claims, how these protections are abused, and the broader impact on genuine LGBTQ asylum seekers. Real-life examples and potential policy reforms are also discussed to address these vulnerabilities while preserving the integrity of the system.

Introduction

In recent years, Canada and other Western countries have become safe havens for individuals from marginalized communities who face persecution in their home countries. Among these groups, LGBTQ+ individuals are particularly vulnerable, often suffering discrimination, violence, and in some cases, severe legal consequences, simply because of their sexual orientation or gender identity. In recognition of these threats, many nations have introduced asylum pathways that offer protection to those who face persecution due to their LGBTQ+

status. However, this compassionate policy has also attracted individuals who falsely claim LGBTQ+ identity in order to obtain refugee status, exploiting an asylum system designed to help those in genuine need.

This chapter delves into the misuse of LGBTQ+ refugee claims, exploring how individuals fabricate their identity and the consequences of such fraudulent behavior. We will discuss specific examples of how this exploitation takes place, the challenges faced by immigration authorities, and the broader implications for genuine LGBTQ+ refugees and asylum systems as a whole.

The LGBTQ+ Asylum Pathway

Countries like Canada, the United States, and several European nations offer specific protection pathways for LGBTQ+ individuals facing persecution. These pathways are rooted in the belief that people deserve the freedom to express their identity without fear of harm or legal repercussions. In many parts of the world, LGBTQ+ individuals face severe threats—ranging from physical violence to imprisonment or even execution—due to their sexual orientation or gender identity. For this reason, Western countries have taken steps to create safe pathways for asylum, aiming to uphold fundamental human rights and provide refuge to those who have nowhere else to turn.

LGBTQ+ refugee claims are typically based on personal narratives that detail experiences of discrimination, threats, and harm in the individual's home country. Asylum officers assess these claims by interviewing applicants, evaluating their narratives, and determining whether the fear of persecution is credible and well-founded. The very personal nature of

LGBTQ+ persecution makes these claims particularly difficult to verify. Unlike other asylum cases, where documentation of political activities or involvement in conflicts might be available, LGBTQ+ claims often rely heavily on personal testimonies. This reliance on narrative-based evidence creates opportunities for exploitation by those seeking to take advantage of the system.

Exploitation of LGBTQ+ Claims

The humanitarian approach that underpins LGBTQ+ asylum policies is unfortunately also what makes them vulnerable to fraud. There have been numerous instances where individuals have falsely claimed to be LGBTQ+ to gain refugee status, using fabricated stories of persecution to exploit the system.

Misrepresentation and Fabrication of Identity

One of the primary methods of exploitation involves misrepresentation or the fabrication of an LGBTQ+ identity. Individuals seeking to immigrate to countries like Canada may choose to falsely claim they are gay, lesbian, bisexual, or transgender, knowing that this could increase their chances of being granted asylum. These individuals often create elaborate backstories detailing how they were persecuted in their home countries due to their sexual orientation. They may claim experiences such as social ostracization, threats from family or community members, or even physical harm, in an attempt to present a compelling case for asylum.

For instance, there have been documented cases of applicants who, after being denied entry through other immigration pathways, chose to reapply for asylum by claiming to be part of the LGBTQ+ community. In one such example, an individual applied for asylum citing political persecution, but when that claim was rejected, the person re-applied with a new story, this time claiming to be gay and facing persecution in their home country. During the subsequent interviews, inconsistencies in the individual's story raised red flags, and immigration officials began to suspect that the LGBTQ+ claim was fabricated purely as a last resort to secure entry.

Coaching and Assistance from Third Parties

In many cases, individuals attempting to exploit LGBTQ+ asylum pathways receive coaching from smugglers, legal advisors, or even friends who have successfully navigated the system. These third parties provide applicants with detailed instructions on what to say during interviews, how to describe their experiences, and how to portray their identity convincingly. This kind of coaching makes it even more challenging for asylum officers to distinguish between genuine and fraudulent claims, especially when the applicant appears well-prepared and presents a consistent narrative.

One example involved a group of individuals who, before seeking asylum, were coached extensively on how to present themselves as gay in front of immigration authorities. They were given specific instructions on how to dress, what kind of language to use, and what kinds of stories would sound believable to asylum officers. These individuals were also advised to join LGBTQ+ support groups and attend events as a way to bolster their claims. While some of them were successful in securing asylum, their deception ultimately came to light when authorities investigated discrepancies in their stories and community ties.

Challenges Faced by Immigration Authorities

The fraudulent use of LGBTQ+ claims pose significant challenges for immigration authorities. Unlike other types of asylum claims, which may involve documentary evidence or witness testimonies, LGBTQ+ claims are deeply personal and often rely on narratives that are difficult to verify. Immigration officers are tasked with assessing not only the credibility of the individual's story but also the authenticity of their identity—a process that can be both intrusive and ethically complex.

In many cases, asylum officers rely on interviews to determine the validity of an LGBTQ+ claim. They look for consistency in the applicant's story, their understanding of LGBTQ+ experiences, and evidence that supports their fear of persecution. However, fraudulent applicants who have been well-coached can often present convincing stories, making it challenging for officers to discern the truth. The use of coaching and fabricated backstories undermines the credibility of genuine claims, making it more difficult for those who are truly in need to receive protection.

Moreover, the fear of discrimination and cultural stigma often makes it challenging for genuine LGBTQ+ applicants to share their experiences openly. Many LGBTQ+ individuals come from countries where they have had to hide their identity for their entire lives. Asking them to prove their sexual orientation or gender identity in a short interview can be traumatic, and the fear of being disbelieved can prevent them from presenting their stories fully. Fraudulent claims add another layer of complexity, creating an environment in which genuine refugees may face increased scrutiny and skepticism.

Broader Implications for Genuine Refugees

The exploitation of LGBTQ+ asylum pathways has significant implications for genuine refugees. The presence of fraudulent claims erodes the credibility of LGBTQ+ asylum seekers as a whole, leading to increased skepticism among asylum officers and the public. When fraudulent cases come to light, they often attract significant media attention, which in turn shapes public perception and can lead to more restrictive immigration policies.

Stricter Requirements and Increased Scrutiny

As authorities become aware of the potential for fraud, they may respond by implementing stricter requirements and subjecting all LGBTQ+ asylum seekers to greater scrutiny. This increased scrutiny can be traumatizing for genuine applicants, who may already be reluctant to discuss their experiences due to the stigma surrounding LGBTQ+ identity in their home countries. Stricter requirements may also mean that genuine refugees are asked to provide evidence that they simply do not have, such as photographs, social media activity, or witness statements attesting to their sexual orientation. For individuals who have spent their lives hiding their identity, these requirements can be impossible to meet.

For example, a genuine LGBTQ+ asylum seeker from a conservative country might have no documented history of LGBTQ+ relationships or community involvement, simply because any evidence would have put their life at risk. When asked to provide such evidence, they may struggle to meet the requirements, leading to delays or even denials of their claims. In contrast, fraudulent applicants who have been coached may be more adept at fabricating the evidence needed, further complicating the assessment process.

Impact on Community Trust and Integration

The presence of fraudulent claims also has an impact on community trust and integration efforts. LGBTQ+ refugee support groups and community organizations play a crucial role in helping new arrivals settle into their host countries, providing them with emotional support, resources, and a sense of belonging. However, the misuse of these pathways can lead to mistrust within these communities, as members become wary of individuals who may be pretending to be LGBTQ+ for personal gain.

In one documented case, a local LGBTQ+ support group discovered that an individual they had been assisting was not genuinely gay, but had fabricated their story to gain asylum. The discovery led to a sense of betrayal and suspicion within the group, making it harder for them to trust new members. This mistrust can create barriers for genuine refugees who need support, ultimately hindering their ability to integrate and thrive in their new environment.

Policy Considerations and Recommendations

Addressing the issue of fraudulent LGBTQ+ asylum claims requires a careful balance between ensuring that genuine refugees receive the protection they need and preventing abuse of the system. Immigration authorities must be equipped with the tools and training necessary to identify fraudulent claims without compromising the dignity and privacy of genuine applicants.

Specialized Training for Asylum Officers

One recommendation is to provide specialized training for asylum officers on LGBTQ+ issues, cultural nuances, and the specific challenges faced by LGBTQ+ individuals in different parts of the world. By understanding the unique experiences of LGBTQ+ refugees, officers can better assess the credibility of claims and identify potential red flags. Training should also focus on conducting interviews in a way that is respectful and non-intrusive, creating a safe space for genuine applicants to share their stories.

Collaboration with LGBTQ+ Organizations

Collaboration with LGBTQ+ organizations can also be an effective way to support the assessment of asylum claims. These organizations have expertise in LGBTQ+ issues and can provide valuable insights into the challenges faced by refugees. By working with community groups, immigration authorities can gain a better understanding of the specific threats faced by LGBTQ+ individuals and receive guidance on how to evaluate claims in a culturally sensitive manner.

Enhanced Screening and Verification Procedures

While it is important to avoid intrusive questioning, there are steps that immigration authorities can take to enhance the screening process for LGBTQ+ asylum claims. This could include cross-referencing information provided by applicants with available records, conducting multiple interviews to assess consistency, and using behavioral analysis techniques to identify discrepancies. It is also crucial that authorities verify the authenticity of supporting documents, such as membership in LGBTQ+ organizations, to ensure that they are not fabricated.

Conclusion

The exploitation of LGBTQ+ asylum pathways is a complex issue that poses significant challenges for immigration authorities and genuine refugees alike. While fraudulent claims represent a small percentage of overall asylum applications, their impact is profound, undermining the credibility of LGBTQ+ asylum seekers and placing additional barriers in the path of those in genuine need of protection.

Addressing these challenges requires a multifaceted approach that includes specialized training for asylum officers, collaboration with LGBTQ+ organizations, and enhanced verification procedures. By taking these steps, immigration authorities can better protect the integrity of LGBTQ+ asylum pathways while ensuring that those who genuinely need refuge receive the protection they deserve. Ultimately, the goal is to create a system that is both compassionate and secure, upholding the rights of LGBTQ+ individuals while preventing exploitation.

Chapter Thirteen: Espionage and Influence Operations

This chapter delves into the covert use of legal immigration pathways by foreign governments, criminal networks, and terrorist organizations to infiltrate Western countries. We will explore how agents enter as students, business investors, or skilled professionals, then engage in espionage and influence operations to gather intelligence, manipulate public opinion, and interfere in political processes. By examining real-world cases and identifying common tactics, this chapter sheds light on the strategic objectives behind these operations and the complex challenges they pose for national security. We'll also discuss policy measures that can help mitigate these threats while maintaining the integrity of immigration systems.

Introduction

The use of legal immigration pathways by foreign governments, criminal organizations, and other malign actors to infiltrate host countries is not merely a theoretical threat; it has become a complex reality in today's globalized world. Through espionage and influence operations, these actors aim to gather sensitive intelligence, shape public opinion, exert political influence, and disrupt the host nation's social and political stability. Unlike overt acts of aggression, espionage and influence operations are covert and often utilize ordinary immigration pathways to grant agents the cover and legitimacy needed to integrate within the target country. This chapter delves into the specific tactics and objectives behind these operations, their historical and modern instances, and the unique challenges they present for host nations.

We'll examine how espionage and influence operations function, explore real-life examples of such activities, and analyze how these covert actions exploit weaknesses in immigration pathways. The chapter will also explore the complex role of social media and technology in enhancing the reach and effectiveness of influence operations and conclude with recommendations for how governments can adapt their policies and resources to mitigate these risks.

Understanding Espionage and Influence Operations

Espionage and influence operations serve as instruments for foreign actors to subtly advance their interests in target countries. Espionage involves the covert gathering of intelligence, often focusing on government policies, military capabilities, technological developments, and economic strategies. Influence operations, on the other hand, aim to manipulate public opinion, shape discourse, and sway political or social movements, usually to create environments favorable to the foreign actor's goals.

These operations fall into four primary categories:

1. **Traditional Espionage** – Intelligence collection by covert agents or "sleeper cells" embedded in key institutions or industries.

2. **Economic Espionage** – Targeted theft or compromise of intellectual property, trade secrets, and research for economic gain.
3. **Social Influence Operations** – Manipulation of public opinion or discourse through social media, public figures, or educational institutions.
4. **Political Influence Operations** – Attempts to influence or destabilize the political landscape of the target country through funding, media manipulation, or interference in elections.

The individuals involved in these activities are often granted entry into the host country through legal means, blending into society as students, professionals, business investors, or family members. Once integrated, they can operate with relative freedom and limited oversight, making it challenging for authorities to detect their true intentions.

Pathways for Entry and Infiltration

The immigration pathways used by agents for espionage and influence operations vary widely, but there are common patterns in how these pathways are exploited:

1. **Student Visas and Research Placements**
   Academic institutions are frequently targeted for infiltration. Agents can enter under student or research visas, granting them access to cutting-edge research, scientific collaboration, and intellectual property. Often, these individuals are embedded in fields such as nuclear physics, artificial intelligence, biotechnology, and cybersecurity. Academic environments also provide

access to young minds and future leaders, allowing foreign actors to subtly influence students' perspectives on political and social issues.

2. **Employment-Based Immigration Programs**

   Foreign governments and organizations often embed agents in employment-based programs to gain access to sensitive industries like defense, telecommunications, and information technology. This access allows them to gather intelligence on proprietary technologies and critical infrastructure, and in some cases, to develop networks of influence within key sectors.

3. **Investment and Business Visas**

   Through investment visas and business fronts, agents can establish local companies, gain credibility in the business community, and create networks of local allies. These companies may serve as fronts for intelligence gathering, influence operations, or money laundering activities that fund future operations.

4. **Cultural or Diplomatic Exchange Programs**

   Cultural and diplomatic exchange programs, including those sponsored by embassies, often grant foreign agents a platform to influence public opinion and cultivate networks within host countries. Cultural events, language schools, and arts programs allow them to reach local communities and promote narratives favorable to their home government.

Examples of Espionage and Influence Operations

Numerous real-world examples illustrate the scope and impact of espionage and influence operations:

1. **The Confucius Institutes**

   Confucius Institutes, which are Chinese cultural centers embedded in universities worldwide, have been scrutinized for their potential role in spreading pro-China narratives and monitoring Chinese students and scholars abroad. These institutes offer language and cultural programs but have been accused of promoting Chinese government views, restricting academic freedom, and discouraging criticism of Chinese policies. Some governments, including those of the United States and Australia, have restricted or closed Confucius Institutes over concerns about influence and academic independence.

2. **Russian Interference in Western Elections**

   Russian agents and operatives have reportedly used social media and local media outlets to influence elections in the United States and Europe. Through troll farms, social media bots, and targeted disinformation campaigns, these operatives seek to exploit social divisions and encourage distrust in democratic institutions. Many have argued that the 2016 U.S. election was marked by substantial evidence of Russian interference, including the release of a series of secret documents aimed at influencing voter behavior and inciting social unrest.

3. **Economic Espionage in Silicon Valley**

   Chinese operatives have been reported to infiltrate American tech companies in Silicon Valley, often gaining employment through legitimate channels or creating business fronts. Once embedded, these individuals allegedly engage in economic espionage by stealing intellectual property, trade secrets, and technology, providing an economic advantage to Chinese companies and state-run enterprises. This pattern has led the FBI and the U.S. Department of Justice to launch numerous investigations and prosecutions related to technology theft.

4. **Iranian Influence in the Middle East and Europe**
   Iran's Islamic Revolutionary Guard Corps (IRGC) is known to operate influence networks throughout the Middle East and in Europe. Through religious and cultural organizations, Iranian agents work to advance pro-Iranian narratives, support proxy groups, and recruit local populations. These networks often target Shi'a communities, aiming to increase Iran's influence and counter Western interests in the region.

Tactics Employed in Influence Operations

Influence operations are designed to remain covert while subtly shaping the target country's internal dynamics. The following tactics are commonly used:

1. **Media Manipulation and Disinformation**
   Through online platforms, fake news websites, and social media accounts, foreign agents create narratives that align with their interests. These narratives can range from politically divisive content to anti-government propaganda aimed at eroding trust in democratic institutions. By exploiting existing social issues, these operations intensify social discord and increase polarization.

2. **Social Media Bots and Troll Farms**

   Automated bots and troll farms amplify certain narratives by flooding social media platforms with repetitive messages, false information, and inflammatory content. These techniques make it appear as if certain viewpoints have wide support, swaying public opinion and making it harder for individuals to discern fact from fiction.

3. **Funding Political Campaigns and Lobbying**

   Foreign entities often funnel money into political campaigns, nonprofits, or lobbying efforts to gain influence over local politics. This funding can be used to promote politicians who are sympathetic to their interests or to influence public policy in their favor. While the use of foreign funds in political campaigns is restricted in many countries, covert funding networks enable foreign actors to bypass these regulations.

4. **Cultivating and Recruiting Local Assets**

   Agents frequently target locals who have access to valuable information or social networks, building relationships to leverage for future operations. These locals may be unaware they are being used as assets in an influence operation, especially if the approach is gradual and based on shared ideological beliefs.

Challenges in Detecting and Countering Espionage and Influence Operations

Espionage and influence operations are difficult to detect and counter due to their covert nature and the legitimate appearance of those involved. Immigration pathways provide these operatives with access to society and allow them to operate under legal protections.

1. **Difficulty in Identifying Covert Operatives**
   Individuals engaged in espionage or influence operations often possess all necessary documentation, making it challenging to distinguish them from legitimate immigrants. Furthermore, the agencies responsible for vetting visa applications often lack the resources or specialized training needed to identify covert operatives among the general immigrant population.

2. **Complexity of Monitoring Influence Operations**
   Influence operations conducted over social media are difficult to trace back to specific actors, as agents often use anonymous accounts, bots, and encrypted communication channels. Social media platforms are only beginning to implement tools to detect coordinated inauthentic behavior, and even these tools may not catch sophisticated operations.

3. **Legal and Ethical Challenges in Surveillance**
   Monitoring suspected operatives often involves surveillance, which raises ethical and legal challenges. Governments must balance national security interests with individuals' right to privacy and freedom of expression. This balance is especially challenging when the agents involved blend seamlessly into civil society, using seemingly lawful means to further their agendas.

Policy Recommendations for Countering Espionage and Influence Operations

Addressing the risks posed by espionage and influence operations requires a multi-pronged approach, focusing on prevention, detection, and response.

1. **Enhanced Security Screening for High-Risk Sectors**
   Immigration pathways that lead to employment in sensitive industries, such as defense, technology, and healthcare, should involve rigorous security screenings, including comprehensive background checks, interviews, and cross-referencing with allied intelligence databases.

2. **Strengthened International Cooperation and Intelligence Sharing**
   Host countries should work closely with allies to share information on known operatives and suspicious entities. Joint efforts between intelligence agencies can provide a more comprehensive understanding of threats, especially when operatives move between multiple countries.

3. **Transparency Requirements for Foreign-Funded Organizations**
   Governments should implement transparency requirements for organizations and institutions that receive foreign funding, especially cultural and educational organizations. These requirements could include mandatory disclosure of funding sources and restrictions on foreign influence in political campaigns.

4. **Digital Literacy Campaigns to Combat Disinformation**
   Education on digital literacy is crucial for the general public to recognize and resist disinformation. Governments, in collaboration with social media platforms, can launch campaigns to educate citizens on

identifying misinformation and understanding how influence operations work.

5. **Legal Reforms to Address Foreign Interference**
Updating legal frameworks to address modern forms of foreign interference, including influence campaigns on social media, can empower law enforcement agencies to investigate and prosecute foreign agents more effectively.

Conclusion

Espionage and influence operations represent a sophisticated, covert threat to national security and social cohesion in host countries. Foreign agents exploit legal immigration pathways to infiltrate key industries, shape public opinion, and influence political landscapes. The insidious nature of these operations requires a proactive, multifaceted response that combines rigorous security measures, international collaboration, and public education. Only through these efforts can host nations protect their sovereignty, maintain social stability, and foster resilience against the covert influence of foreign actors.

Chapter Fourteen: The Rise of Antisemitism in the West: Infiltration, Influence, and Consequences

This chapter explores the alarming rise of antisemitism in Western countries, driven in part by extremist groups infiltrating through immigration pathways. We discuss the influence of these groups on public sentiment, their calls for violence against Jewish communities, and the broader societal impact. The chapter highlights examples of antisemitic incidents, including attacks on synagogues and public demonstrations, while examining how foreign funding and ideological influence contribute to this growing threat. Solutions for addressing the infiltration and countering extremist narratives are also considered.

Introduction

The rise of antisemitism in the West—particularly in Europe, the United States, and Canada—has become a concerning issue in recent years. This surge in hatred against Jewish communities is partly driven by infiltration and influence by certain elements from Islamic countries, particularly those connected to terrorist organizations supported by the Islamic Republic of Iran. This chapter explores the rise of antisemitism in Western countries, its roots in infiltration from groups promoting extremist ideologies, and the tactics used to foster hatred against Jews. It also provides an analysis of the consequences of this growing trend, with particular attention to universities, public demonstrations, and violent attacks on synagogues and Jewish communities.

The chapter also examines how these antisemitic activities are funded and supported through billions of dollars of investment by state sponsors of terrorism. This includes the financial and ideological backing provided by Iran to groups like Hezbollah, Hamas, and Islamic Jihad, which have contributed to spreading hatred and violence against Jews, even far beyond the Middle East. Finally, we will discuss potential policy measures and community actions to mitigate and counter the rise of antisemitism, thereby fostering safer and more inclusive societies.

The Roots of Antisemitism in the West

Antisemitism in the West has a long and dark history. However, the recent rise can be attributed to new dynamics involving the infiltration of extremist ideologies and influences from actors connected to the Islamic Republic of Iran and other state sponsors of terrorism. Since the early 2000s, there has been a marked increase in antisemitic incidents across Europe and North America, ranging from verbal abuse and hate speech to physical violence against individuals and attacks on Jewish institutions.

One of the primary contributors to this growing trend is the spread of extremist ideologies brought by individuals affiliated with groups that have infiltrated the West under the guise of asylum seekers, students, or legal immigrants. These groups often carry the agenda of the terrorist organizations they are affiliated with—organizations funded and supported by Iran and other hostile actors. The influence of these extremist elements is especially evident in environments like universities, where hateful rhetoric against Jews is often framed as political activism.

The Role of Iranian Influence and State-Sponsored Terrorist Groups

The Islamic Republic of Iran has long been known as one of the leading state sponsors of terrorism worldwide. Through billions of dollars of funding, Iran has supported numerous groups such as Hezbollah, Hamas, the Islamic Jihad, and the Houthis in Yemen. These groups have consistently propagated extreme anti-Israel and antisemitic ideologies. The ideological influence of these groups has not remained confined to the Middle East; it has infiltrated Western nations through various avenues, often taking advantage of the freedoms and rights granted in democratic societies.

Many of the individuals connected to these groups have entered Western countries, posing as legitimate refugees, students, or immigrants. Once settled, they work to spread their extremist ideologies, often targeting Jewish communities. For example, elements affiliated with Hezbollah or Hamas have used the platform of university student organizations to spread antisemitic propaganda, mask hatred under the banner of free speech, and call for the elimination of the state of Israel—all while exploiting the legal and social protections offered by Western democracies.

Public Demonstrations and Calls for Violence

One of the most visible manifestations of this trend has been the rise in public demonstrations where antisemitic chants and calls for violence have been openly expressed. The slogan "From the river to the sea, Palestine will be free" has become a common refrain at many anti-Israel rallies. While often framed as a political statement, this slogan implicitly calls for the elimination of Israel and has been linked to calls for violence against Jews.

In some European cities, such as Amsterdam and Berlin, demonstrators have openly called for intifada—a term associated with violent uprisings against Jews—and have chanted for the destruction of Israel. These public displays of hatred are not isolated incidents; rather, they are organized events often connected to extremist networks. The participation of individuals with affiliations to terrorist organizations in these demonstrations underscores the role of external influence in driving antisemitism in the West.

Attacks on Jewish Institutions and Individuals

The rise of antisemitism in the West has led to a surge in attacks on Jewish institutions, including synagogues, schools, and community centers. These attacks are often carried out by individuals who have been radicalized either directly by terrorist organizations or through the influence of extremist propaganda. In several high-profile incidents, attackers have targeted synagogues during services, leading to tragic loss of life and creating an atmosphere of fear within Jewish communities.

In addition to attacks on institutions, there has also been an increase in street-level assaults on Jewish individuals. In cities across Europe and North America, Jews have been targeted simply for wearing religious symbols, such as the kippah. In one widely reported incident in Amsterdam, a group of extremists attacked a Jewish man on the street, shouting antisemitic slurs and praising terrorist organizations. Such incidents highlight the growing danger faced by Jewish communities as a result of the spread of extremist ideologies.

The Role of Universities in Promoting Antisemitic Ideologies

Universities have long been seen as bastions of free thought and open debate, but they have also become breeding grounds for antisemitic ideologies in recent years. Student groups affiliated with extremist organizations have used the cover of academic freedom to promote hate speech against Jews and call for the destruction of Israel. Events such as "Israeli Apartheid Week" have become common on many campuses, where speakers openly espouse antisemitic rhetoric, demonize Jewish students, and create a hostile environment for anyone who supports Israel.

These activities are often funded by external sources, including organizations with ties to hostile foreign governments. The influence of these groups on campuses is particularly concerning, as it helps normalize antisemitic attitudes among young people and create an atmosphere where hatred against Jews is seen as a legitimate form of political expression. Jewish students have reported feeling increasingly unsafe on campuses, with many facing harassment and intimidation for their beliefs or for simply being Jewish.

Exploiting Freedoms in Western Democracies

One of the reasons that antisemitic elements have been able to flourish in the West is the exploitation of freedoms that are foundational to democratic societies. Freedom of speech, freedom of assembly, and human rights protections are all vital components of Western democracies, but they can also be manipulated by those with malicious intent. Extremist elements have taken advantage of these freedoms to spread hatred and incite violence, knowing that their actions are often protected under the guise of free expression.

For example, extremist speakers who openly call for violence against Jews or the destruction of Israel are often invited to speak at public events or universities. These individuals exploit the protection of free speech to spread their hateful ideologies, while at the same time silencing those who oppose them through intimidation and harassment. This abuse of democratic freedoms presents a significant challenge for Western nations, as they seek to balance the protection of free speech with the need to prevent incitement to violence.

Suggested Solutions to Combat Antisemitism

Addressing the rise of antisemitism in the West requires a comprehensive and multi-faceted approach that involves governments, educational institutions, civil society, and law enforcement. Below are several key recommendations for combating this growing problem:

1. **Stronger Law Enforcement and Intelligence Cooperation**: Western countries must strengthen intelligence-sharing and law enforcement cooperation to identify and monitor individuals with ties to terrorist organizations who may be spreading extremist ideologies. This includes enhancing border security measures to prevent individuals with extremist ties from entering under the guise of legitimate immigration or refugee claims.

2. **Enforcement of Hate Speech Laws**: Governments should enforce existing hate speech laws to prevent the open incitement of violence against Jews. While protecting freedom of speech is crucial, there must be clear limits when speech crosses the line into incitement

to violence. Authorities should hold individuals and organizations accountable for promoting antisemitic rhetoric that leads to violence.

3. **Oversight of Foreign Funding**: It is essential to increase transparency and oversight of foreign funding for organizations operating in the West, particularly those connected to universities and student groups. Governments should require full disclosure of foreign donations and take action against organizations found to be promoting hatred or supporting extremist activities.

4. **Educational Initiatives**: Schools and universities should implement educational programs that promote tolerance and provide a balanced perspective on the Israeli-Palestinian conflict. Universities should also ensure that all students feel safe on campus, regardless of their background or beliefs. This includes taking a firm stand against harassment and intimidation directed at Jewish students.

5. **Support for Jewish Communities**: Governments and civil society must work together to support Jewish communities facing threats. This includes increased funding for security at Jewish institutions, as well as providing resources for victims of antisemitic attacks. Community outreach programs can also help foster greater understanding and solidarity between different groups, reducing the sense of isolation often felt by Jewish communities.

6. **Designation of Terrorist Organizations**: As seen in Canada and the United States, designating organizations

like the IRGC as terrorist entities can limit their ability to operate and raise funds in Western countries. The European Union should also consider similar designations to close the doors to individuals and groups with ties to extremist activities, preventing them from entering and spreading their ideologies.

Conclusion

The rise of antisemitism in the West, driven in part by infiltration and influence from extremist elements connected to state sponsors of terrorism, represents a significant challenge for Western nations. This growing trend threatens not only Jewish communities but also the core values of tolerance and inclusivity that underpin democratic societies. By exploiting democratic freedoms, these extremist groups have been able to spread hatred, incite violence, and create an atmosphere of fear for Jewish individuals in Europe, the United States, and Canada.

Addressing this issue requires a determined and coordinated response from governments, law enforcement, educational institutions, and civil society. By strengthening intelligence cooperation, enforcing hate speech laws, increasing oversight of foreign funding, and supporting educational initiatives, Western nations can work to counter the rise of antisemitism and protect the safety and dignity of Jewish communities. The challenge is significant, but with a comprehensive approach, it is possible to turn the tide against hatred and ensure that all individuals can live free from fear and persecution.

Chapter Fifteen: Case Study: The Islamic Republic of Iran Agents in Canada

This chapter provides an extensive analysis of how agents linked to the Islamic Republic of Iran have strategically infiltrated Canada through legal immigration channels. The primary focus is on the Islamic Revolutionary Guard Corps (IRGC), a paramilitary organization that wields significant economic and political power in Iran and is designated as a terrorist organization by both Canada and the United States. We will examine the IRGC's motivations for infiltrating Western nations, particularly Canada, the methods they use to enter the country, and documented cases of their covert activities. This chapter will also explore the broader implications of Iranian state-sponsored infiltration for Canadian national security and propose measures to strengthen immigration policies and intelligence cooperation. Given the evolving geopolitical landscape, we will also assess the potential impact of the European Union's consideration to designate the IRGC as a terrorist organization, which could significantly curb the ability of Iranian operatives to exploit legal immigration pathways.

Introduction

Canada's open immigration policies, strong rule of law, and commitment to multiculturalism have made it an attractive destination for immigrants from diverse backgrounds. However, these same characteristics make Canada vulnerable to exploitation by hostile foreign states seeking to expand their influence and conduct covert operations. Among these, the Islamic Republic of Iran, through its powerful and clandestine arm, the IRGC, has been one of the most active in utilizing Canada's legal immigration channels to establish a foothold.

The IRGC, an elite branch of the Iranian military, operates as both a security force and a political-economic conglomerate. Its influence extends beyond Iran's borders, where it engages in intelligence gathering, financial manipulation, and influence operations. Canada's designation of the IRGC as a terrorist organization, along with similar designations by the United States, underscores the seriousness of the threat. This chapter will examine the IRGC's strategic objectives in infiltrating Canada, the methods used, specific cases of Iranian agents operating within the country, and the broader implications for national and allied security.

Strategic Objectives of the IRGC in Canada

The IRGC's activities in Canada are driven by a combination of intelligence gathering, influence operations, financial objectives, and efforts to suppress opposition to the Iranian regime. These strategic goals are aligned with Iran's broader geopolitical ambitions and reflect the IRGC's role as a key instrument of state power.

1. **Intelligence Gathering and Espionage**
    The IRGC's primary objective in infiltrating Canada is to gather intelligence on political, economic, and military developments. Canada's close alliance with the United States, its participation in NATO, and its advanced technology sectors make it a valuable target for Iranian espionage. The IRGC seeks to collect sensitive information on Canadian foreign policy, economic sanctions, and technological innovations, which can be used to bolster Iran's strategic capabilities.

2. **Influence Operations and Shaping Public Opinion**
    The IRGC engages in influence operations aimed at shaping public discourse and policy debates in Canada. By establishing or infiltrating cultural and religious organizations, the IRGC can disseminate pro-regime propaganda and counter negative narratives about Iran. These efforts are aimed at softening Canada's stance on economic sanctions and human rights issues, while also attempting to sway the opinions of Iranian-Canadians.

3. **Sanctions Evasion and Financial Manipulation**
    With significant economic sanctions imposed on Iran by Western nations, the IRGC has turned to Canada as a potential hub for circumventing these restrictions. Through front companies and real estate investments, the IRGC can launder funds, move assets covertly, and generate revenue streams that support its military and intelligence operations. The financial freedom offered by Canada's robust banking system and lenient investment

policies has made it an attractive target for these activities.

4. **Targeting and Suppressing Dissidents**

   Canada is home to a large Iranian diaspora, including many critics of the regime. The IRGC actively monitors these communities, targeting activists, journalists, and dissidents who speak out against the Iranian government. Using intimidation tactics and surveillance, IRGC agents aim to silence opposition voices and deter anti-regime activities within Canada. This not only undermines the safety of Iranian-Canadians but also threatens the broader principle of free expression in a democratic society.

Methods of Infiltration

The IRGC has exploited several legal immigration pathways to place agents within Canada. These methods take advantage of Canada's investment visas, student visas, family reunification programs, and skilled worker pathways, allowing Iranian operatives to enter under the guise of legitimate immigration. The tactics employed are sophisticated and often involve the use of forged documents, front organizations, and manipulation of the legal system.

1. **Investment and Business Visas**

   The IRGC frequently uses investment-based immigration programs to gain residency in Canada. These programs, designed to attract wealthy investors, are vulnerable to misuse due to limited oversight. IRGC operatives set up front companies, make significant real estate investments, and present themselves as legitimate business owners. This strategy not only facilitates entry but also provides a cover for laundering money and conducting financial operations.

Example: A network of IRGC-linked individuals used Canada's investor visa program to establish multiple businesses. Although these companies appeared legitimate, investigations revealed that they were involved in transferring funds back to Iran, bypassing international sanctions. The businesses acted as fronts, allowing operatives to integrate into the Canadian financial system while carrying out covert activities.

2. **Student and Academic Visas**

   Canada's higher education system is a prime target for IRGC infiltration. Iranian agents often enter the country as students or visiting scholars, gaining access to advanced research and technologies. Academic environments provide an ideal setting for operatives to blend in, build networks, and gather sensitive information on dual-use technologies that could be repurposed for military applications.

Example: Several Iranian nationals enrolled in Canadian universities were later found to be affiliated with research institutions linked to the Iranian military. These individuals collected data on nuclear technology and cyber defense systems, sending the information back to Iran. The incident highlighted vulnerabilities in the vetting process for student visas and raised concerns about technology transfer risks.

3. **Family Reunification Programs**

   The IRGC has exploited Canada's family reunification program by using fraudulent documents to claim familial ties with Iranian-Canadians. This method allows agents to enter the country legally and establish themselves within local communities. Once in Canada, they can conduct surveillance on Iranian dissidents and engage in influence operations.

Example: An individual claiming to be a spouse of a Canadian citizen entered the country using forged documents. After settling in a major Canadian city, the individual was discovered to be an IRGC operative who was actively monitoring and reporting on anti-regime activists.

4. **Religious and Cultural Organizations**

   The IRGC often uses religious and cultural organizations as fronts for its influence operations. These organizations, which receive funding from pro-regime entities, host events that promote the Iranian government's narrative. They also serve as hubs for gathering intelligence on the Iranian-Canadian community and identifying potential targets for recruitment.

Example: Several mosques and cultural centers across Canada were found to have connections to Iranian state-affiliated groups. These centers hosted events that glorified the Iranian regime while subtly promoting disinformation campaigns aimed at countering criticisms of Iran's policies.

Challenges Faced by Canadian Authorities

1. **Resource Constraints and Limited Expertise**
   Canadian immigration and intelligence agencies face challenges in thoroughly vetting applicants from high-risk regions. The volume of applications, combined with the sophisticated tactics used by the IRGC, often overwhelms available resources, making it difficult to detect infiltration.

2. **Diplomatic Limitations**
   Canada's severed diplomatic relations with Iran since 2012 have hindered efforts to verify the authenticity of documents and background information for Iranian applicants. Without direct communication channels, Canadian authorities must rely on limited intelligence-sharing agreements with allies, complicating the vetting process.

3. **Balancing National Security with Civil Liberties**
   Enhanced surveillance and stringent checks could improve detection of foreign operatives but also raise ethical concerns about racial profiling and privacy violations. Striking a balance between security and civil rights remains a significant challenge.

Policy Recommendations

1. **Stricter Screening for High-Risk Applicants**
   Canada should implement comprehensive background checks, enhanced interviews, and financial audits for applicants from countries designated as state sponsors of

terrorism, such as Iran. This would involve greater scrutiny of investment and business visa applications to detect potential IRGC affiliations.

2. **Enhanced Collaboration with International Partners**
   Increasing data-sharing agreements with the United States, United Kingdom, and other allies can help identify and track high-risk individuals attempting to enter Canada. Intelligence-sharing about known IRGC operatives and affiliated entities would bolster Canadian efforts to prevent infiltration.

3. **Sanctions and Legal Restrictions on IRGC Affiliates**
   Canada should strengthen enforcement of targeted sanctions against IRGC-linked individuals and entities, including freezing assets and imposing travel bans. If the European Union proceeds with designating the IRGC as a terrorist organization, coordinated sanctions could further limit the IRGC's ability to exploit Western immigration systems.

4. **Support and Protection for Iranian Dissidents**
   Providing additional legal and security support for Iranian-Canadian dissidents can help counteract intimidation tactics used by the IRGC. Establishing a special task force within Canadian law enforcement to handle threats against activists would enhance protection for those targeted by the regime.

Conclusion

The case study of Iranian infiltration into Canada illustrates the complex challenge of countering state-sponsored espionage and influence operations. By exploiting legal immigration pathways, the IRGC has managed to establish a presence in Canada that threatens national security, compromises public trust, and endangers the Iranian-Canadian diaspora. A coordinated response involving enhanced immigration screening, international intelligence cooperation, and targeted legal measures is essential to safeguard Canada's sovereignty and maintain the integrity of its immigration system.

Chapter Sixteen: Policy and Security Measures

This chapter explores the comprehensive policy and security measures necessary to counter the exploitation of immigration pathways and safeguard national security. It addresses the need for a holistic approach, balancing rigorous screening with humanitarian obligations, and emphasizes the importance of international collaboration, advanced technology, and intelligence integration. We will examine specific policy reforms that countries have implemented or are considering, the role of enhanced vetting procedures, and the importance of inter-agency and international cooperation. The chapter also highlights the complexities of implementing these measures while maintaining the integrity and accessibility of immigration systems for genuine applicants.

Introduction

Immigration has always been a cornerstone of national development, contributing to cultural diversity, economic growth, and social cohesion. However, as we have explored in previous chapters, legal immigration pathways are increasingly vulnerable to exploitation by malicious actors, including foreign state agents, criminal networks, and terrorist organizations. The misuse of these channels poses significant risks to national security, public safety, and the integrity of immigration systems.

To address these challenges, governments must adopt a multi-faceted policy response that integrates enhanced vetting processes, technological advancements, and international intelligence collaboration. This chapter provides an in-depth analysis of the necessary policy and security measures to prevent infiltration, protect genuine immigrants, and strengthen the resilience of immigration systems against exploitation.

Enhanced Vetting and Screening Procedures

One of the most critical components of preventing infiltration through legal immigration pathways is the implementation of enhanced vetting and screening procedures. These measures are designed to identify high-risk individuals before they gain entry, reducing the likelihood of exploitation by foreign agents or criminal elements.

1. **Comprehensive Background Checks and Identity Verification**

Comprehensive background checks are fundamental to assessing the risk posed by applicants. This process involves verifying personal information, criminal history, and any connections to known terrorist organizations or criminal networks. In cases where applicants originate from conflict zones or authoritarian regimes with unreliable records, immigration authorities may need to rely on biometric data and advanced verification tools.

Example: The United States has implemented an enhanced vetting process for visa applicants from high-risk countries, requiring additional documentation and interviews. The process includes cross-referencing applicant data with intelligence databases to identify individuals with potential ties to terrorist groups or hostile foreign states.

2. Biometric Screening and Digital Identification

The use of biometric screening, such as fingerprints, facial recognition, and iris scans, has become a key tool in preventing identity fraud and detecting multiple applications under different identities. Biometric data provides a reliable way to verify the identity of applicants, particularly those coming from regions with limited or compromised record-keeping.

Example: The European Union's Eurodac system uses fingerprint data to track asylum seekers across member states, reducing the risk of "asylum shopping" and helping authorities detect individuals who attempt to file multiple applications under different names. This system has proven effective in preventing fraudulent claims and enhancing the integrity of the immigration process.

3. Social Media and Digital Footprint Analysis

In today's digital age, analyzing an applicant's online presence and social media activity can provide valuable insights into their background and intentions. Immigration authorities are increasingly using these tools to detect inconsistencies in applicants' stories, identify potential red flags, and verify the authenticity of claims made during the application process.

Example: Several Western countries, including Canada and the United Kingdom, have begun using social media analysis as part of their vetting procedures. This approach helps identify individuals who may be attempting to conceal extremist views or affiliations with hostile organizations.

Inter-Agency Coordination and Intelligence Sharing

Effective immigration policy requires seamless coordination between immigration authorities, law enforcement agencies, and intelligence services. The complexity of modern threats demands a comprehensive approach that integrates data and insights from multiple sources.

1. Establishing Centralized Immigration Databases

A centralized immigration database that consolidates information from various government agencies can significantly improve the efficiency of screening processes. Such databases enable real-time access to relevant data, including criminal records, visa histories, and intelligence reports, helping authorities make informed decisions about applicants.

Example: The United States' ESTA (Electronic System for Travel Authorization) system allows immigration and customs authorities to pre-screen travelers before they arrive. By cross-referencing applicant data with law enforcement and intelligence databases, ESTA can identify high-risk individuals and prevent them from boarding flights to the U.S.

2. Enhanced Collaboration with Intelligence Agencies

Close collaboration between immigration authorities and national intelligence agencies is crucial for identifying individuals with potential ties to terrorist organizations or hostile foreign states. Intelligence agencies can provide detailed information about high-risk applicants, including known associates, travel patterns, and connections to state-sponsored espionage or influence operations.

Example: In response to concerns about foreign infiltration, the Five Eyes Alliance—comprising the U.S., Canada, the U.K., Australia, and New Zealand—has strengthened intelligence-sharing agreements focused on immigration-related threats. These agreements facilitate the exchange of data on known operatives and high-risk individuals, helping member countries detect and prevent infiltration.

3. International Data-Sharing Agreements

Given the global nature of migration, international cooperation is essential to combat cross-border threats. Data-sharing agreements between countries allow for the exchange of information about visa applicants, including biometric data, criminal records, and travel histories. Such agreements are particularly important for monitoring individuals from high-risk regions who may attempt to exploit immigration systems in multiple countries.

Example: The European Union's Schengen Information System (SIS) enables member states to share information about individuals who pose a threat to public safety or national security. This system helps track the movements of high-risk individuals across borders and enhances the ability of member states to respond quickly to potential threats.

Policy Reforms and Legislative Measures

Addressing the vulnerabilities in immigration systems requires not only enhanced screening and intelligence collaboration but also robust policy reforms and legislative measures. These changes can help close loopholes, increase transparency, and deter malicious actors from exploiting immigration pathways.

1. **Stricter Investment Visa Regulations**

Investment-based immigration programs are particularly vulnerable to misuse, as they often involve large financial transactions with limited oversight. Strengthening the regulatory framework for these programs can reduce the risk of exploitation by individuals or organizations seeking to launder money or gain residency for ulterior motives.

Policy Recommendation: Implement mandatory financial audits for applicants of investment visas, including verification of the source of funds and enhanced scrutiny of investments in high-risk sectors. Countries should also consider limiting access to sensitive industries, such as technology and defense, for individuals entering through investment-based pathways.

2. **Mandatory DNA Testing for Family Reunification Applications**

Family reunification programs are prone to abuse through the submission of fraudulent documentation. Introducing mandatory DNA testing in high-risk cases can help verify the authenticity of familial relationships and prevent individuals from using fake documents to gain entry.

Policy Recommendation: Establish clear guidelines for when DNA testing is required, focusing on applicants from regions with high rates of document fraud or known vulnerabilities. This measure should be implemented with careful consideration of privacy concerns and in compliance with international human rights standards.

3. **Legal Designation of State-Sponsored Entities as Terrorist Organizations**

Legal designations play a crucial role in limiting the ability of state-sponsored entities, such as the IRGC, to exploit immigration systems. By designating such groups as terrorist organizations, countries can impose stricter sanctions, freeze assets, and prevent associated individuals from entering the country.

Example: Canada's designation of the IRGC as a terrorist organization has provided a legal basis for enhanced screening and enforcement actions against individuals linked to the group. The United States has maintained a similar designation for years, and the European Union is considering following suit, which could further restrict the IRGC's activities in the West.

Balancing Security and Humanitarian Responsibilities

While enhancing immigration security is critical, it is equally important to ensure that reforms do not unduly burden genuine applicants or violate human rights. Striking the right balance between rigorous screening and maintaining an accessible, compassionate immigration system requires a nuanced approach.

1. Transparency and Public Accountability

Governments should maintain transparency in the implementation of new screening measures, providing clear information to the public about the reasons for policy changes and their expected impact. This helps build public trust and reduces fears of discrimination or undue restrictions on immigration.

2. Support for Genuine Refugees and Immigrants

Enhanced screening procedures must be complemented by robust support systems for genuine refugees and immigrants, including access to legal assistance, mental health services, and community integration programs. Providing these resources helps mitigate the potential negative impacts of stricter vetting processes on vulnerable populations.

Conclusion

In a world where immigration systems are increasingly targeted by malicious actors, implementing comprehensive policy and security measures is essential to protect national sovereignty and public safety. Enhanced vetting, inter-agency coordination, international data-sharing, and targeted policy reforms are critical components of a resilient immigration strategy. By balancing security needs with a commitment to humanitarian values, countries can strengthen their defenses against exploitation while continuing to welcome those who seek safety and new opportunities in good faith. As we move forward, it is vital for policymakers to remain vigilant, adapt to emerging threats, and ensure that immigration remains a source of strength and diversity for nations around the world.

Part III: The Broader Implications and Future Directions

Chapter Seventeen: The Social and Economic Costs of Immigration Fraud and Espionage

This chapter examines the far-reaching social and economic consequences of immigration fraud and espionage. While previous chapters have explored how legal immigration pathways can be exploited, this chapter delves into the broader impact of such abuses on host countries. We will analyze the economic burdens placed on social services, the erosion of public trust, the effects on national security, and the unintended consequences for genuine immigrants. The chapter highlights how fraudulent activities not only strain government resources but also contribute to social polarization, undermining the integration of legitimate immigrants and fueling anti-immigrant sentiments.

Introduction

The phenomenon of immigration fraud and espionage extends beyond individual cases of deception; it represents a significant threat to the fabric of society and the stability of national economies. As immigration systems are exploited by individuals with malicious intent, host countries face mounting social and economic costs. These costs manifest in various ways, from increased public spending on immigration enforcement and welfare services to the disruption of social cohesion and heightened national security risks.

The impacts of immigration fraud and espionage are compounded by the growing complexity of global migration patterns and the sophistication of state-sponsored operations. While countries must uphold their commitments to humanitarian principles and open borders, they also face the challenge of mitigating the detrimental effects of exploitation. This chapter explores the tangible and intangible costs of immigration fraud and espionage, offering a comprehensive analysis of how these activities undermine public trust, drain resources, and affect the lives of both citizens and genuine immigrants.

Economic Costs of Immigration Fraud

The economic ramifications of immigration fraud are extensive, affecting government budgets, social services, and the broader economy. Fraudulent activities place an immense burden on public systems, diverting resources away from legitimate needs and creating inefficiencies.

1. **Increased Costs for Immigration Enforcement and Processing**

Immigration fraud necessitates significant government spending on enforcement and verification processes. Authorities must allocate substantial resources to investigate fraudulent claims, conduct background checks, and carry out legal proceedings. These efforts divert funds away from other critical services and contribute to a backlog in immigration processing, affecting both genuine and fraudulent applicants.

Example: In Canada, a surge in fraudulent asylum claims in the mid-2010s led to a significant increase in spending on immigration enforcement and legal processes. The need for additional investigations and court hearings placed a heavy burden on the immigration system, leading to delays and increased operational costs.

2. **Strain on Social Services and Welfare Programs**

Fraudulent immigration claims can place undue pressure on social services, including housing, healthcare, and welfare programs. Individuals who gain entry under false pretenses may be eligible for public benefits, straining systems designed to support vulnerable populations. This diversion of resources reduces the availability of services for genuine refugees and low-income residents, exacerbating social inequalities.

Example: In several European countries, including Germany and Sweden, fraudulent asylum claims during the height of the refugee crisis overwhelmed public services. Local governments faced challenges providing adequate housing and medical care, leading to overcrowded shelters and stretched healthcare systems.

3. Economic Impact of Money Laundering Through Investment Programs

Investment-based immigration programs, when exploited for money laundering, can distort local economies. Influxes of illicit funds into real estate markets and business investments inflate property prices, making it difficult for local residents to afford housing. Additionally, these activities can undermine financial regulations and erode investor confidence, affecting the overall stability of the economy.

Example: In major cities like London, New York, and Vancouver, there have been documented cases of property markets being inflated by foreign investment tied to laundered money. The artificial demand created by these illicit investments has driven up housing prices, displacing local communities and creating economic instability.

Social Costs of Immigration Fraud and Espionage

Beyond the economic implications, immigration fraud and espionage have profound social impacts. These activities erode public trust, fuel xenophobia, and hinder the successful integration of legitimate immigrants, leading to a fractured and polarized society.

1. Erosion of Public Trust in Immigration Systems

High-profile cases of immigration fraud and espionage can significantly damage public perception of immigration systems. When citizens believe that immigration policies are being exploited, it fosters skepticism and reduces support for welcoming newcomers. This erosion of trust can lead to calls for stricter immigration controls, which may inadvertently harm genuine applicants who depend on these pathways for safety and opportunity.

Example: In the United States, widespread media coverage of visa fraud cases linked to criminal networks has led to increased public skepticism of immigration programs like the H-1B visa. Public pressure has resulted in policy changes and more stringent vetting processes, which, while necessary, have also contributed to longer wait times and reduced access for legitimate skilled workers.

2. Increased Xenophobia and Social Tensions

The perception of widespread immigration fraud can exacerbate xenophobic attitudes and contribute to social polarization. Host communities may begin to view all immigrants with suspicion, regardless of their background or intentions. This negative perception undermines efforts to build inclusive communities and can lead to discrimination, harassment, and even violence against immigrants.

Example: In several European countries, including Italy and Hungary, political movements have capitalized on fears of immigration fraud and infiltration, using these issues to promote anti-immigrant rhetoric. The resulting polarization has deepened social divisions, making it more difficult for immigrants to integrate and for communities to foster mutual understanding.

3. Impact on Genuine Immigrants and Refugees

The fallout from immigration fraud often falls hardest on genuine immigrants and refugees, who may face increased scrutiny, longer processing times, and a more hostile environment. Policy changes aimed at curbing fraud, such as stricter documentation requirements and heightened security screenings, can place additional burdens on those fleeing persecution or seeking a better life.

Example: In Canada, policy reforms introduced to combat fraudulent family sponsorships have led to increased requirements for documentation and verification. While these measures help prevent exploitation, they have also made it more difficult for legitimate families to reunite, causing emotional distress and prolonged separation.

National Security Implications

Immigration fraud and espionage are not only economic and social issues but also pose significant national security risks. The infiltration of hostile actors through legal immigration pathways can undermine national sovereignty and compromise sensitive information.

1. Threats to Critical Infrastructure and Cybersecurity

Agents who enter a country through fraudulent means may gain access to critical industries, including technology, defense, and energy. Once embedded, they can engage in espionage, sabotage, or cyberattacks, targeting vital infrastructure and sensitive information. The consequences of such activities can be devastating, affecting national security and economic stability.

Example: Several Western nations have reported incidents of cyber-espionage linked to foreign operatives who gained residency or employment through fraudulent visa applications. These individuals were found to have accessed sensitive data related to defense projects and critical infrastructure, posing a serious threat to national security.

2. Influence Operations and Political Interference

State-sponsored actors often use legal immigration channels to infiltrate host countries and engage in influence operations. By leveraging their status as residents or citizens, they can establish networks, fund political campaigns, and manipulate public opinion. Such activities can undermine democratic processes and weaken trust in government institutions.

Example: Intelligence agencies in the United States and Europe have uncovered efforts by foreign governments to use legal immigrants as part of broader influence campaigns. These operatives have been involved in spreading disinformation, funding advocacy groups, and attempting to sway public opinion on key policy issues.

3. Undermining of Allied Security Cooperation

When one country's immigration system is exploited, it can have ripple effects on its allies. For instance, individuals who gain citizenship or residency in one country may use their new status to travel freely within allied nations, bypassing stricter security checks. This loophole can compromise the collective security of international coalitions, such as NATO or the European Union.

Example: The ease of travel for citizens within the Schengen Area has raised concerns about individuals who obtain EU citizenship through fraudulent means. These individuals can move freely across member states, complicating efforts to track and monitor potential threats.

Policy Recommendations to Mitigate Social and Economic Costs

Addressing the social and economic impacts of immigration fraud requires targeted policy interventions and a collaborative approach among nations.

1. Public Awareness Campaigns

Educating the public about the risks and realities of immigration fraud can help counter misinformation and reduce xenophobia. Transparent communication about policy reforms and enforcement efforts can build public trust and foster a more informed dialogue on immigration issues.

2. Increased Funding for Immigration Enforcement

Governments should allocate additional resources for immigration enforcement, including specialized fraud detection units and advanced investigative tools. Enhanced funding can improve the capacity of immigration authorities to detect and prevent fraud, reducing the strain on social services and minimizing the economic burden.

3. Stronger International Collaboration

Effective management of immigration fraud requires robust international cooperation. Countries should strengthen data-sharing agreements, collaborate on best practices, and support joint enforcement initiatives to identify and combat cross-border threats.

Conclusion

The social and economic costs of immigration fraud and espionage are profound, affecting public trust, social cohesion, and national security. As host countries grapple with these challenges, it is essential to adopt a balanced approach that addresses the root causes of exploitation while preserving the integrity of immigration systems. By implementing comprehensive policy reforms, enhancing international cooperation, and fostering public understanding, nations can protect their borders, support genuine immigrants, and uphold the values that make immigration a vital part of modern society.

Chapter Eighteen: Balancing Openness with Security

This chapter explores the fundamental tension between maintaining open and welcoming immigration systems and the need to safeguard national security. It examines the delicate balance policymakers must strike when developing immigration policies that are both inclusive and secure. We will discuss the challenges of implementing stringent security measures without compromising the humanitarian principles that underpin modern immigration systems. Additionally, the chapter will explore how countries can design policies that deter malicious actors while still honoring their commitments to protect refugees and facilitate legal immigration. Drawing on real-world examples, we will analyze strategies that countries have employed to address these dual objectives, as well as the trade-offs and potential unintended consequences of various approaches.

Introduction

Immigration has always played a crucial role in shaping societies, contributing to economic growth, cultural diversity, and global interconnectedness. Many nations, particularly in the West, have built their identities on principles of openness, freedom, and the opportunity for newcomers to start a new life. However, in an era of rising geopolitical tensions, increased transnational crime, and sophisticated state-sponsored infiltration, maintaining open borders and generous immigration policies has become increasingly challenging.

Governments face the difficult task of designing immigration systems that are both inclusive and secure. The pressure to tighten borders and implement more rigorous screening processes often conflicts with humanitarian obligations and the economic benefits of immigration. This chapter explores how countries can navigate this complex landscape, striving to uphold their core values while addressing legitimate security concerns.

The Benefits of Openness in Immigration Policy

Openness in immigration policy is not merely a humanitarian gesture; it is a strategic approach that can yield significant economic, social, and cultural benefits. Countries that welcome immigrants often experience growth and dynamism, driven by the skills, innovation, and diverse perspectives that newcomers bring.

1. Economic Growth and Innovation

Immigrants play a critical role in driving economic growth, filling labor shortages, and contributing to the development of new industries. Many of the world's most successful entrepreneurs and innovators have immigrant backgrounds, and immigration has been shown to increase productivity and stimulate investment.

Example: In the United States, immigrants are more likely than native-born citizens to start businesses. These businesses create jobs and contribute to the economy, with immigrant-owned companies generating billions of dollars in revenue each year. The tech industry, in particular, relies heavily on skilled foreign workers, many of whom enter through employment-based immigration programs.

2. Cultural Diversity and Social Enrichment

Immigration contributes to cultural diversity, bringing new traditions, languages, and ideas that enrich the social fabric of host countries. This diversity fosters creativity and innovation, as people from different backgrounds collaborate and share unique perspectives.

Example: In cities like Toronto, London, and Sydney, vibrant immigrant communities have become integral to the cultural landscape. These cities are known for their multicultural festivals, international cuisine, and inclusive neighborhoods, all of which enhance the quality of life for residents.

3. Strengthening Diplomatic and International Relations

Welcoming immigrants and refugees can strengthen a country's international standing, enhancing its reputation as a leader in human rights and global cooperation. By providing refuge to those fleeing persecution, countries demonstrate their commitment to humanitarian values, which can foster goodwill and strengthen diplomatic ties.

Example: During the Syrian refugee crisis, Germany's decision to accept a large number of refugees was seen as a powerful humanitarian gesture, boosting the country's global image. Although the policy faced domestic challenges, it reinforced Germany's commitment to international solidarity and human rights.

The Challenges of Ensuring Security

While the benefits of openness are substantial, they must be weighed against the growing security risks associated with immigration. Malicious actors, including state-sponsored operatives, terrorist organizations, and criminal networks, have exploited legal immigration pathways to gain entry to host countries. These threats necessitate robust security measures, but implementing such measures without undermining the integrity and accessibility of immigration systems is a complex challenge.

1. The Threat of Infiltration by Malicious Actors

As discussed in earlier chapters, individuals affiliated with foreign governments, terrorist groups, or criminal organizations have used legal immigration channels, such as investment visas, employment-based visas, and family reunification programs, to infiltrate Western countries. These actors pose significant risks, engaging in espionage, influence operations, and illicit activities that threaten national security.

Example: Several Western intelligence agencies have reported cases of foreign operatives entering through legal immigration pathways, later engaging in activities such as cyber-espionage, intellectual property theft, or attempts to influence political processes. The exploitation of student and research visas by individuals seeking access to sensitive technology has also been a growing concern.

2. Public Perception and Political Pressure

High-profile cases of immigration fraud or security breaches can lead to public outcry and increased political pressure to tighten immigration controls. Politicians may respond with restrictive measures that, while intended to enhance security, can also have negative consequences for genuine immigrants and refugees.

Example: In the wake of terrorist attacks involving individuals with immigrant backgrounds, several countries have enacted stricter immigration policies, including travel bans and enhanced vetting procedures for applicants from certain regions. While these measures aim to address security concerns, they have also sparked debates about discrimination, civil liberties, and the impact on legitimate applicants.

3. Balancing Privacy with Enhanced Screening

Enhanced screening procedures, such as biometric data collection, social media monitoring, and extensive background checks, can help detect high-risk individuals. However, these measures raise concerns about privacy and civil liberties. Immigration authorities must navigate the delicate balance between protecting national security and respecting the rights of applicants.

Example: The European Union has faced challenges in implementing comprehensive biometric screening measures due to stringent privacy laws. While these measures can enhance security, the legal and ethical implications of mass data collection have sparked significant debate, particularly in countries with strong privacy protections.

Strategies for Balancing Openness and Security

To achieve a balance between openness and security, countries must adopt a strategic approach that leverages technology, international cooperation, and policy innovation. The goal is to design systems that deter exploitation without undermining the principles of fairness, inclusivity, and human rights.

1. Risk-Based Screening and Vetting Procedures

Rather than applying a one-size-fits-all approach, countries can implement risk-based screening procedures that focus resources on high-risk applicants. By prioritizing enhanced checks for individuals from conflict zones or regions with known security concerns, authorities can streamline processing for low-risk applicants while maintaining rigorous oversight where it is needed most.

Policy Recommendation: Develop a tiered vetting system that categorizes applicants based on risk level, with additional screening for those flagged as high-risk. This approach allows for efficient resource allocation and reduces delays for genuine low-risk applicants.

2. Leveraging Advanced Technology for Enhanced Security

Artificial intelligence (AI) and machine learning can play a critical role in detecting patterns of fraud and identifying high-risk individuals. These technologies can analyze vast amounts of data, cross-referencing information from multiple sources to flag inconsistencies or suspicious activity that may indicate fraud or security threats.

Policy Recommendation: Invest in AI-driven analytics tools to support immigration authorities in processing applications efficiently and identifying potential red flags. Ensure that the implementation of such technologies complies with privacy laws and ethical guidelines to maintain public trust.

3. Strengthening International Collaboration and Intelligence Sharing

The global nature of migration and the interconnectedness of national security demands robust international cooperation. Countries must work together to share intelligence, harmonize screening protocols, and jointly monitor high-risk individuals. By collaborating with allies, countries can enhance their ability to detect and prevent threats that exploit immigration pathways.

Policy Recommendation: Expand data-sharing agreements between allied nations, focusing on high-risk individuals and emerging threats. Create joint task forces to monitor cross-border activities and coordinate responses to potential security risks.

4. Transparent Communication and Public Education

To maintain public support for immigration policies, governments must communicate transparently about the measures they are implementing and the reasons behind them. Public education campaigns can help dispel myths, reduce fear, and foster a more nuanced understanding of immigration issues.

Policy Recommendation: Launch public information campaigns that explain the economic and social benefits of immigration, the security measures in place, and the efforts being made to prevent exploitation. Engaging with communities and addressing concerns directly can help build trust and support for balanced immigration policies.

Conclusion

Balancing openness with security is a complex but essential task for modern immigration policy. By embracing the benefits of immigration while implementing targeted, risk-based security measures, countries can protect their national interests without sacrificing their core values. The path forward requires innovation, international cooperation, and a commitment to upholding human rights. As we navigate these challenges, it is crucial to remember that a secure and inclusive immigration system is not only possible but necessary for building strong, resilient, and diverse societies. Through thoughtful policy design and strategic implementation, nations can continue to welcome newcomers, protect public safety, and thrive in an increasingly interconnected world.

Chapter Nineteen: Solutions and Recommendations

This chapter outlines practical solutions and policy recommendations to address the vulnerabilities in immigration systems that have been exploited by fraudulent actors, state-sponsored agents, and criminal networks. By analyzing the weaknesses identified in previous chapters, this chapter provides a comprehensive framework for reform. We will explore how enhanced verification processes, technological innovations, international cooperation, and public policy adjustments can strengthen immigration pathways while maintaining humanitarian commitments. Each recommendation is designed to strike a balance between safeguarding national security and ensuring the system remains accessible to genuine refugees and immigrants. The chapter also includes real-world examples of how certain strategies have been implemented successfully to mitigate risks.

Introduction

The complexities of modern immigration systems make them susceptible to various forms of exploitation, from fraudulent asylum claims to strategic infiltration by state-sponsored operatives. Addressing these challenges requires a multifaceted approach that combines strong legal frameworks, advanced technology, effective enforcement, and international collaboration. The solutions must be comprehensive and proactive, capable of adapting to evolving threats while preserving the core values of openness and compassion that underpin immigration policies.

This chapter presents a series of recommendations aimed at reinforcing the integrity of immigration systems. These solutions are designed to close existing loopholes, streamline processes, and enhance oversight, thereby reducing the opportunities for exploitation. By adopting these strategies, countries can build more resilient immigration systems that protect both national security and the rights of legitimate immigrants.

Enhancing Verification and Screening Processes

One of the primary areas of concern in immigration systems is the verification of applicants' identities, qualifications, and backgrounds. Weaknesses in screening processes have allowed individuals with fraudulent claims or malicious intent to gain entry. Strengthening verification measures is essential to prevent exploitation.

Implementing Advanced Biometric Screening

Biometric data, such as fingerprints, facial recognition, and iris scans, offer a highly reliable method of verifying identities. By integrating biometric screening into immigration processes, countries can reduce the risk of identity fraud and multiple applications under different aliases. This technology can be particularly effective in detecting applicants who attempt to exploit humanitarian pathways by presenting false identities.

Example: In one European country, biometric screening at border entry points was instrumental in identifying a group of individuals who had used forged passports to claim asylum. The biometric data revealed that they had previously applied under different names in multiple countries, helping authorities uncover the deception and prevent further abuse of the asylum system.

Utilizing Blockchain for Document Verification

Blockchain technology can be employed to create a secure, tamper-proof digital ledger for verifying educational credentials, professional qualifications, and identity documents. By using blockchain, immigration authorities can cross-check applicant information against verified records, reducing the likelihood of forged documents being accepted.

Recommendation: Establish partnerships between immigration agencies and educational institutions to implement blockchain-based verification of academic credentials. This approach ensures that only genuine qualifications are accepted, minimizing the risk of fraud.

Expanding Background Checks for High-Risk Applicants

Enhanced background checks should be mandatory for applicants from regions with high rates of document fraud or known links to terrorist organizations and criminal networks. These checks should include social media analysis, financial audits, and consultation with intelligence databases to identify potential red flags.

Example: In the United States, enhanced background checks have been effective in identifying individuals linked to extremist groups who attempted to enter the country through student visa programs. The checks revealed ties to known operatives, leading to the denial of their applications and preventing potential security breaches.

Leveraging Technology and Data Analytics

The use of technology in immigration processing has the potential to transform screening and detection capabilities. By integrating artificial intelligence (AI), machine learning, and big data analytics, immigration authorities can more effectively identify patterns of fraud and detect high-risk individuals.

AI-Driven Risk Assessment Systems

AI and machine learning algorithms can analyze large datasets to identify patterns indicative of fraud or malicious intent. These systems can flag applications for further review based on anomalies, such as inconsistent travel history, sudden changes in financial status, or discrepancies in declared information.

Example: In one Asian country, an AI-driven system was used to analyze visa applications, detecting a network of fraudulent businesses that had been created solely to sponsor individuals with no real job prospects. The system flagged these applications for manual review, leading to the discovery of an organized scheme aimed at bypassing immigration regulations.

Real-Time Data Sharing Among Allied Nations

Data sharing between allied nations is crucial for tracking high-risk individuals who may attempt to exploit immigration systems in multiple countries. By sharing intelligence and immigration data in real time, countries can detect patterns of asylum shopping, visa fraud, and potential infiltration by hostile actors.

Recommendation: Establish a secure, international data-sharing platform for immigration agencies, enabling instant cross-referencing of applicant information against known watchlists and databases maintained by intelligence agencies.

Using Blockchain for Secure Tracking of Applications

Blockchain technology can also be applied to track the progress of immigration applications securely. This approach reduces the risk of tampering and provides a transparent audit trail, making it easier to detect unauthorized changes or fraudulent activity within the application process.

Strengthening Legal Frameworks and Enforcement Mechanisms

Robust legal frameworks are essential for preventing and addressing immigration fraud and exploitation. By enacting clear, enforceable regulations and ensuring that immigration authorities have the tools needed for effective enforcement, countries can deter malicious actors and maintain the integrity of their systems.

Introducing Penalties for Employers Involved in Visa Fraud

Employers who knowingly sponsor fraudulent applicants or misrepresent job requirements contribute to the exploitation of employment-based immigration pathways. Introducing strict penalties, including heavy fines and criminal charges, for employers involved in such activities can serve as a strong deterrent.

Example: In a case uncovered in a North American country, a technology firm was found to have sponsored dozens of foreign workers with falsified credentials. The company faced substantial fines and was barred from sponsoring visas for a decade, sending a clear message about the consequences of circumventing immigration laws.

Implementing Cessation and Revocation Policies for Fraudulent Applications

Cessation hearings and revocation policies allow immigration authorities to withdraw residency or citizenship status from individuals who are found to have obtained it fraudulently. These measures are crucial for addressing cases where individuals misrepresent their need for asylum or fabricate familial relationships to gain entry.

Recommendation: Establish a standardized process for cessation hearings, with clear criteria and procedures for revoking status in cases of proven fraud. This approach can help maintain the integrity of the immigration system while ensuring that only genuine applicants retain their legal status.

Harmonizing Immigration Laws Across Jurisdictions

Inconsistent immigration laws between countries can create loopholes that are easily exploited by transnational criminal organizations and state-sponsored agents. Harmonizing key aspects of immigration law across allied nations can help close these gaps and reduce opportunities for exploitation.

Recommendation: Develop multilateral agreements focused on standardizing critical elements of immigration law, including vetting procedures, eligibility criteria, and enforcement mechanisms.

Fostering International Cooperation and Capacity Building

Global migration patterns and the interconnected nature of modern threats require a collaborative, international response. By enhancing cooperation and capacity building among countries, immigration systems can be strengthened to better manage the risks associated with fraud and infiltration.

Establishing Joint Task Forces for Immigration Fraud

Joint task forces comprising immigration authorities, law enforcement, and intelligence agencies can be effective in investigating and disrupting complex immigration fraud schemes. These task forces can operate across borders, pooling resources and expertise to tackle transnational threats.

Example: A joint task force between several European nations successfully dismantled a human trafficking ring that had been using forged documents to bring individuals into the EU under the guise of family reunification. The coordinated effort allowed for simultaneous raids and arrests across multiple countries.

Capacity Building for High-Risk Regions

Many immigration fraud cases originate from regions with limited administrative capacity and weak governance structures. By providing support and resources to these countries, host nations can help improve local document verification processes, reducing the incidence of fraud at the source.

Recommendation: Launch international aid initiatives focused on improving civil registration and identity verification systems in conflict-affected and high-risk countries.

Developing Global Standards for Immigration Security

Establishing global standards for immigration security, including best practices for screening, verification, and data protection, can help create a unified approach to managing risks. These standards should be regularly updated to reflect evolving threats and technological advancements.

Conclusion

The challenges posed by immigration fraud and infiltration are significant, but they are not insurmountable. By implementing a combination of enhanced verification processes, advanced technology, stronger legal frameworks, and international cooperation, countries can build more resilient immigration systems. These solutions not only help prevent exploitation but also ensure that immigration remains a force for good, contributing to economic growth, cultural diversity, and global stability. Moving forward, policymakers must continue to adapt and innovate, embracing strategies that protect national security while honoring the values of openness, compassion, and inclusivity.

Chapter Twenty: A Path Forward: Safeguarding Refugee Rights and National Security

This concluding chapter seeks to outline a comprehensive vision for the future of immigration policy, one that balances the dual imperatives of protecting national security and upholding the humanitarian principles that underpin refugee and immigration systems. As we have explored throughout this book, the vulnerabilities in these systems have been exploited by malicious actors, threatening both public safety and the integrity of the processes designed to offer refuge to those in need. This chapter will present a roadmap for reform, focusing on policy recommendations, strategic innovations, and a framework for international cooperation. By integrating security measures with a commitment to human rights, we can forge a path forward that safeguards national interests while providing a lifeline to those fleeing persecution and violence.

Introduction

In a world increasingly defined by conflict, geopolitical tensions, and transnational threats, immigration policy has become a focal point of debate and reform. Governments are grappling with the challenge of welcoming newcomers while ensuring that immigration systems are not exploited by individuals and groups with malicious intent. This balancing act is complex and fraught with difficult trade-offs, but it is also essential. The future of immigration policy must be grounded in both security and compassion, recognizing the value that immigrants and refugees bring while implementing robust measures to protect national interests.

This chapter presents a vision for an immigration system that is resilient, fair, and adaptable. It draws on lessons from previous chapters and provides detailed recommendations for creating a balanced framework that addresses the root causes of exploitation while maintaining the humanitarian spirit of refugee protection.

Building a Resilient Immigration System

A resilient immigration system is one that can withstand external pressures, adapt to evolving threats, and respond effectively to emerging challenges. To achieve this, we must first identify the core pillars of resilience: robust infrastructure, comprehensive oversight, and the flexibility to adjust policies as needed.

1. **Strengthening Institutional Capacity**

   Many of the vulnerabilities in immigration systems stem from a lack of capacity within the institutions responsible for processing applications, conducting background checks, and enforcing regulations. Building stronger institutions with adequate resources, training, and technology is crucial for improving the efficiency and integrity of immigration processes.

   Recommendation: Increase funding for immigration agencies to enhance staffing, provide advanced training on fraud detection, and invest in technology upgrades.

Streamline bureaucratic processes to reduce backlogs and improve the speed and accuracy of decision-making.

2. Adopting a Proactive Approach to Risk Management

Rather than relying solely on reactive measures, immigration systems must adopt a proactive approach to risk management. This involves identifying potential threats before they materialize, using predictive analytics, scenario planning, and early warning systems.

Example: One North American country has implemented a predictive analytics platform that uses historical data on immigration fraud to identify patterns and flag high-risk applications for further review. This proactive approach has significantly reduced the number of fraudulent claims, allowing authorities to focus resources on genuine cases.

3. Establishing a Flexible Policy Framework

A resilient immigration system must be adaptable, capable of adjusting policies and procedures in response to changing circumstances. This flexibility can be achieved through periodic policy reviews, stakeholder consultations, and a willingness to experiment with new approaches.

Recommendation: Introduce a system of regular policy audits, involving feedback from immigration officers, civil society organizations, and affected communities. These audits should assess the effectiveness of current policies and recommend adjustments based on real-world outcomes.

Promoting Transparency and Accountability

Transparency and accountability are fundamental to building public trust in immigration systems. By clearly communicating the goals, processes, and outcomes of immigration policies, governments can foster greater understanding and support from the public while minimizing the potential for exploitation.

1. **Public Reporting and Open Data Initiatives**

   Immigration agencies should publish regular reports on application processing times, approval rates, and fraud detection statistics. Open data initiatives that provide anonymized information about the outcomes of immigration applications can help increase transparency and allow independent researchers to identify trends and areas for improvement.

   Example: A European country has launched an open data portal that provides detailed information on immigration applications, including approval rates by country of origin, processing times, and reasons for denial. This transparency has improved public confidence in the system and helped identify discrepancies that may indicate areas of concern.

2. **Independent Oversight Bodies**

Establishing independent oversight bodies can help ensure that immigration policies are implemented fairly and effectively. These bodies should have the authority to investigate complaints, conduct audits, and recommend reforms based on their findings.

Recommendation: Create an independent immigration ombudsman office with a mandate to oversee the processing of applications, address public concerns, and provide an impartial assessment of the effectiveness and fairness of immigration policies.

3. **Enhanced Public Communication Strategies**

Governments must engage in open dialogue with the public about the benefits and challenges of immigration. Effective communication strategies can help counter misinformation, address concerns, and highlight the contributions of immigrants to society.

Example: In response to rising anti-immigrant sentiment, a Western government launched a public awareness campaign that featured stories of successful immigrant entrepreneurs and highlighted the economic and cultural contributions of newcomers. The campaign helped shift public opinion, increasing support for inclusive immigration policies.

Integrating Advanced Technology for Improved Security

Technological advancements offer significant potential to enhance the security of immigration systems while streamlining processes for genuine applicants. By leveraging innovations in artificial intelligence, blockchain, and data analytics, governments can create more efficient and secure immigration pathways.

1. **AI-Powered Fraud Detection Systems**

Artificial intelligence can analyze vast amounts of application data, cross-referencing information from multiple sources to detect inconsistencies and identify potential fraud. Machine learning algorithms can be trained to recognize patterns indicative of deceptive behavior, flagging high-risk applications for further investigation.

Example: An Asian country has implemented an AI-powered system that scans visa applications for signs of fraud, using indicators such as discrepancies in financial documents, travel history inconsistencies, and unusual patterns of sponsorship. The system has significantly reduced processing times and improved detection rates.

2. **Blockchain for Secure Document Verification**

Blockchain technology can be used to create a tamper-proof digital ledger for verifying documents submitted by immigration applicants. By providing a secure, transparent method of document verification, blockchain can help reduce the incidence of forged credentials and false claims.

Recommendation: Develop a blockchain-based platform for document verification, integrated with educational institutions, employers, and government agencies to ensure that all submitted credentials are authentic and traceable.

3. **Enhanced Data Analytics for Risk Assessment**

Big data analytics can help immigration authorities assess the risk level of applicants by analyzing trends and patterns in application data. By identifying correlations between certain risk factors and fraudulent behavior, authorities can better allocate resources and focus on high-risk cases.

Strengthening International Cooperation and Multilateral Agreements

Given the global nature of migration and the interconnectedness of security threats, international cooperation is essential for building a robust immigration system. Multilateral agreements and collaborative frameworks can help harmonize policies, facilitate information sharing, and enhance joint enforcement efforts.

1. **Creating Regional Immigration Security Networks**

Regional security networks that involve immigration agencies, law enforcement, and intelligence services can help monitor cross-border threats and share real-time information about high-risk individuals and emerging fraud schemes.

Example: A group of countries in the Middle East and North Africa has established a regional immigration security network that shares biometric data and intelligence reports. This collaboration has improved the detection of fraudulent documents and reduced the movement of individuals linked to criminal organizations.

2. Standardizing Vetting Procedures Across Allied Nations

Standardizing vetting procedures, including background checks and biometric screening, across allied nations can help close loopholes and reduce opportunities for exploitation. Consistent standards also facilitate smoother processing for genuine applicants, reducing duplication of efforts.

Recommendation: Develop an international agreement on standardized vetting procedures for immigration, with a focus on high-risk applicants and sectors prone to exploitation.

3. Capacity Building for Source Countries

Many issues in immigration systems originate in source countries with weak administrative infrastructure. By investing in capacity building, such as improving civil registration systems and training local officials, host countries can help reduce the incidence of fraud at its source.

Conclusion

Creating a balanced, secure, and compassionate immigration system is a complex but achievable goal. The path forward requires a holistic approach that integrates advanced technology, robust legal frameworks, enhanced institutional capacity, and strong international cooperation. By implementing the solutions outlined in this chapter, countries can address the vulnerabilities that have been exploited by malicious actors while preserving the integrity and accessibility of immigration pathways for genuine refugees and immigrants.

The future of immigration policy lies in its ability to adapt, innovate, and remain true to the core values of openness and protection for the vulnerable. Through thoughtful reform and proactive measures, we can build an immigration system that is not only resilient in the face of threats but also a beacon of hope and opportunity for those seeking a better life.

Part IV: Economic Refugees and Irregular Migration

Chapter Twenty-One: The Southern Border Crisis: Challenges and Exploitation of U.S. Immigration Policies

This chapter explores the ongoing challenges and complexities at the southern border of the United States, which has become both a point of entry for those seeking refuge and an avenue for exploitation by individuals and organizations with malicious intent. We will examine how irregular migration across the U.S.-Mexico border is driven by a variety of factors, such as economic instability, violence, and climate change, and how this chaotic environment is leveraged by criminal organizations and other actors to infiltrate the United States. The chapter will also explore policy loopholes that are exploited by malicious actors, the broader implications for national security and social stability, and provide comprehensive policy recommendations for addressing these critical challenges while safeguarding humanitarian values.

Introduction

The southern border of the United States, shared with Mexico, represents a complex mix of hope, desperation, and strategic challenges. For many, it symbolizes a gateway to a better life—an escape from violence, poverty, and persecution. For others, it has become a vulnerable point that can be exploited for illegal activities, making it a focal point for criminal networks, malicious actors, and individuals seeking to abuse U.S. immigration laws.

This chapter digs into the multifaceted nature of the U.S.-Mexico border crisis, examining the complexities of irregular migration, including the exploitation of asylum procedures and infiltration by criminal organizations. We will explore how the border's vulnerabilities are leveraged by those with malicious intent and analyze the broader implications of this exploitation for national security, public safety, and resource allocation. Ultimately, we seek to understand the fine balance required between protecting legitimate asylum seekers and ensuring the security of the United States.

The Southern Border: A Unique Challenge

The U.S.-Mexico border stretches over 1,900 miles and includes a diverse range of environments: deserts, rivers, mountains, and densely populated urban regions. Each of these landscapes presents unique security challenges. The diversity of this terrain makes effective border management a continuous struggle, despite substantial investments in physical barriers, advanced surveillance, and Border Patrol personnel.

Migration along the southern border is driven by various factors, including economic instability, violence from organized crime, political corruption, and increasingly, climate change. Many of those arriving at the southern border are legitimate asylum seekers fleeing gang violence, political persecution, and poverty in Central American countries, such as Honduras, El Salvador, and Guatemala. Yet, within this context of human desperation lies a darker element—those who exploit the chaos to further illicit activities, undermine public safety, and destabilize communities across the United States.

In addition, the complexity of the U.S. immigration system and the inability to process the overwhelming numbers of migrants in a timely and efficient manner have created a humanitarian and political crisis. As legitimate asylum seekers face extended wait times and live in precarious conditions, the system's weaknesses are exploited by individuals with ulterior motives, often leaving communities across the border ill-equipped to manage the social and economic consequences of uncontrolled migration.

Exploitation of the Asylum System

The United States' asylum system is rooted in humanitarian values, designed to offer protection to individuals fleeing persecution, violence, and other forms of oppression. Under both international and domestic law, the U.S. is obligated to accept asylum claims from those who arrive at its borders seeking protection. However, the sheer volume of asylum seekers arriving at the southern border has placed considerable pressure on the system. Backlogs, limited resources, and insufficient infrastructure have made it nearly impossible to keep up with the demand for processing claims, inadvertently creating opportunities for exploitation.

Criminal networks have adapted quickly to exploit the gaps in the system for financial gain. Smugglers, colloquially known as "coyotes," often charge exorbitant fees to help individuals cross the border, frequently coaching them on what to say during their asylum interviews to improve their chances of gaining entry. In some cases, asylum seekers are provided with scripted stories that are difficult to verify, allowing individuals with fabricated claims to gain access to the United States.

The backlog in processing asylum claims has led to the creation of a de facto "waiting list," with some asylum seekers released into the United States pending a decision on their case. This system, commonly referred to as "catch and release," means that individuals may be allowed to reside in the U.S. for years while waiting for their cases to be adjudicated. Unfortunately, not all individuals who are released into the country report for their scheduled hearings, contributing to an already overwhelmed system. The lack of timely adjudication leaves the door open for exploitation by individuals with malicious intent.

Infiltration by Criminal Organizations

Organized crime has taken full advantage of the vulnerabilities at the southern border to further its operations. Drug cartels, human trafficking rings, and transnational gangs have developed sophisticated strategies to infiltrate the United States, often embedding operatives among large groups of migrants. Mass migration events, such as migrant caravans, provide a perfect opportunity for these organizations to blend in with legitimate asylum seekers.

One of the primary threats posed by this infiltration is the expansion of transnational criminal organizations. Members of criminal gangs, such as MS-13, have been known to cross the border under the guise of seeking asylum. Once inside the United States, they quickly establish or strengthen their criminal operations, contributing to the spread of violence, drug trafficking, and human smuggling.

For example, during times when migrant caravans of thousands move toward the U.S. border, criminal elements have used the mass movement of people as a smokescreen to evade detection by law enforcement. They are able to enter unnoticed alongside families, unaccompanied minors, and legitimate asylum seekers, taking advantage of the confusion and limited resources at border processing facilities. This poses a significant security risk, as once these criminal actors enter the United States, they often operate within vulnerable communities where law enforcement presence is already strained.

Abuse of Legal Loopholes and Policy Challenges

The United States' immigration policies, while rooted in humanitarian ideals, have unintentionally provided avenues for exploitation. Several policy gaps and legal loopholes are frequently abused, allowing individuals with ulterior motives to enter and stay within the country.

One significant policy challenge is the "catch and release" practice, in which individuals apprehended at the border are released into the U.S. while they await immigration proceedings. Due to the extensive backlog in immigration courts, these hearings can take years to be scheduled. During this time, many individuals choose not to report to their hearings and instead disappear into the country, making it nearly impossible for authorities to track them. This loophole is often exploited by those with criminal backgrounds, who use it as an opportunity to evade law enforcement.

Another vulnerability is the abuse of family reunification policies. Under U.S. immigration policy, keeping families together is prioritized. Unfortunately, this well-intentioned policy has been manipulated by criminal networks and individuals seeking entry under false pretenses. There have been documented cases of unrelated adults and children being paired together to pose as family units, making it easier to gain entry. In some cases, criminal organizations have "rented" children to migrants to help them exploit these legal protections. This practice not only undermines the integrity of U.S. immigration policy but also places vulnerable children at extreme risk of exploitation and abuse.

Examples of Infiltration without Specific Names

In one documented case, an individual believed to be associated with a foreign extremist group crossed the southern border and applied for asylum, claiming to be fleeing political persecution. Once granted entry, this individual moved to a major U.S. city and began establishing connections with others from similar backgrounds. Authorities later discovered that the individual was acting on behalf of a foreign extremist group, using their presence in the United States to raise funds, recruit sympathizers, and gather information about potential targets. This case underscores the serious risks posed by individuals who abuse the asylum system to gain entry into the country.

Another example involved a transnational criminal network that used a migrant caravan as a cover to smuggle operatives across the U.S.-Mexico border. These operatives settled in a metropolitan area and began engaging in drug trafficking and money laundering. By taking advantage of the overwhelmed system and the lack of timely processing, these individuals were able to establish themselves in the community and conduct illegal operations before law enforcement became aware of their activities.

Broader Implications for National Security and Social Stability

The consequences of exploiting the southern border extend far beyond immediate security risks. The presence of individuals with malicious intent among legitimate asylum seekers poses significant challenges to national security, public trust, and social stability. When cases of exploitation come to light, they contribute to a broader narrative that questions the integrity of the entire immigration system, leading to increased skepticism and polarization.

The public's perception of asylum seekers and migrants as a whole is often negatively influenced by highly publicized cases of criminal activity or abuse of the system. This perception can lead to a lack of support for immigration reform and a more hostile environment for all newcomers, including those who genuinely need protection and are seeking a better life.

The infiltration of criminal elements also has direct social and economic consequences for U.S. communities. Cities and towns affected by gang violence, drug trafficking, and other criminal activities often experience a higher strain on public resources, including law enforcement, healthcare, and social services. This strain is particularly pronounced in border communities, which may already face economic challenges and lack the infrastructure needed to address a sudden influx of new residents.

The influx of migrants, including legitimate asylum seekers, also places additional pressure on social services such as education, healthcare, and housing. In many cases, border communities are the first point of contact for new arrivals, leading to overcrowded hospitals, schools, and shelters. This strain can further exacerbate tensions between local residents and newcomers, complicating integration efforts and increasing the likelihood of social friction.

Policy Considerations and Recommendations

Addressing the challenges posed by the southern border crisis requires a comprehensive, multifaceted approach that balances the United States' humanitarian obligations with its need to ensure national security. While strengthening border security is an important aspect of managing migration, it is equally essential to close the policy loopholes that allow for exploitation.

One of the most important policy considerations is the need to expedite the asylum process. The United States must increase the number of immigration judges and allocate more resources to adjudicating asylum claims. Reducing the backlog will help ensure that legitimate asylum seekers are processed promptly, while minimizing the opportunity for those with malicious intent to exploit the system. Implementing faster, more efficient processing can reduce the need for practices such as "catch and release," thereby improving overall border management.

Enhanced vetting procedures are also critical. Utilizing advanced biometric screening, conducting thorough background checks, and cross-referencing individuals with international watchlists can help identify high-risk individuals before they are allowed entry. Additionally, ensuring that asylum seekers' stories are carefully reviewed and verified can help prevent false claims from being used as a pathway to entry.

Another key recommendation is to enhance collaboration with Mexico and Central American countries to address the root causes of migration. Many individuals arriving at the southern border are fleeing violence, corruption, and poverty. By investing in development initiatives, anti-corruption programs, and violence prevention efforts in these regions, the United States can help mitigate the push factors that drive migration and reduce the number of people making the dangerous journey north.

Stronger protections must also be put in place for vulnerable populations, particularly children. Rigorous verification of family relationships, the introduction of DNA testing in suspicious cases, and increased protections for unaccompanied minors can help prevent the exploitation of children by criminal networks. By ensuring that children are protected and placed in safe environments, the U.S. can uphold its humanitarian obligations while minimizing opportunities for abuse.

Conclusion

The southern border of the United States is both a symbol of hope and a point of vulnerability. While many individuals arrive seeking safety and the chance to build a better life, others exploit the complexities of the asylum system and the legal loopholes in U.S. immigration policy for malicious purposes. Criminal networks, human traffickers, and foreign operatives leverage these vulnerabilities to infiltrate the country, posing significant risks to national security, public safety, and social stability.

Addressing the challenges of the southern border crisis requires more than just enhanced security measures. A comprehensive approach that includes expedited asylum processing, improved vetting, international collaboration, and robust protections for vulnerable populations is essential. By understanding the complexities of the migration crisis and implementing thoughtful reforms, the United States can ensure its immigration system remains both secure and compassionate, safeguarding the nation's security while upholding its humanitarian values.

Chapter Twenty-Two: Understanding Economic Refugees

This chapter delves into the phenomenon of economic refugees, individuals who migrate primarily to escape poverty and seek better economic opportunities rather than fleeing political persecution or conflict. The distinction between economic refugees and traditional refugees is often blurred, creating challenges for policymakers and immigration systems. Economic migration is driven by complex factors, including economic disparity, globalization, environmental changes, and the pursuit of a better standard of living. This chapter provides a comprehensive analysis of economic refugees, explores the motivations behind their migration, and examines how their presence impacts host countries. We will also discuss the challenges in identifying and categorizing economic refugees and the policy implications for both sending and receiving nations.

Introduction

Global migration patterns have evolved significantly over recent decades, with economic factors playing an increasingly prominent role in shaping the movement of people across borders. While traditional refugees flee due to persecution, violence, or war, a growing number of migrants are driven by economic necessity. These individuals, often referred to as "economic refugees," leave their home countries in search of better job prospects, higher wages, and improved living conditions. Unlike traditional refugees, economic migrants are not necessarily fleeing immediate danger but are escaping economic hardship that may threaten their survival and well-being.

The distinction between economic refugees and traditional refugees is critical yet challenging to make. Economic migration is often influenced by a combination of factors, including weak governance, lack of economic opportunities, environmental degradation, and social instability. For host countries, distinguishing between these motivations is crucial for managing immigration flows, allocating resources, and formulating fair and effective policies.

In this chapter, we will explore the root causes of economic migration, analyze the characteristics of economic refugees, and examine the impact of their movement on both sending and receiving countries. By understanding the dynamics of economic migration, we can better address the policy challenges it poses and find solutions that balance humanitarian concerns with economic realities.

Root Causes of Economic Migration

Economic migration is a complex and multifaceted phenomenon influenced by a variety of push and pull factors. Understanding these root causes is essential for analyzing the motivations behind economic migration and for developing effective responses.

1. **Economic Disparities and Global Inequality**

   One of the primary drivers of economic migration is the vast disparity in income and living standards between countries. In many developing nations, limited job opportunities, low wages, and high levels of poverty push individuals to seek better prospects abroad. The promise of higher wages and a better quality of life in wealthier nations acts as a strong pull factor, drawing economic migrants across borders.

Example: In regions of Sub-Saharan Africa and South Asia, where per capita income remains low, many individuals migrate to Europe or the Middle East in search of employment opportunities. They often work in low-skilled jobs that locals may not want, such as construction, domestic work, or agriculture, sending remittances back home to support their families.

2. **Unemployment and Lack of Economic Opportunities**

High levels of unemployment, particularly among young people, are a significant factor driving economic migration. In countries with weak economies or limited industrialization, the job market may not be able to absorb the growing labor force, leaving many without viable employment options.

Example: In parts of Latin America, where youth unemployment rates are particularly high, many young people migrate northward, seeking work in the United States or Canada. Even if the jobs they find are low-paying, they often provide better wages and stability than what is available in their home countries.

3. **Environmental Degradation and Climate Change**

Environmental factors, including climate change, are increasingly recognized as major drivers of economic migration. Droughts, desertification, rising sea levels, and natural disasters can devastate local economies, particularly those that rely on agriculture or fishing. As livelihoods are disrupted, individuals may be forced to migrate in search of more stable economic environments.

Example: In Southeast Asia, rising sea levels and increased flooding have led to the displacement of communities dependent on coastal agriculture. Many affected individuals migrate to urban areas or seek work abroad as their traditional livelihoods become unsustainable.

4. Political Instability and Poor Governance

While political persecution is a well-known driver of traditional refugee flows, poor governance and political instability can also contribute to economic migration. Corruption, lack of investment in public services, and ineffective economic policies create environments where economic opportunities are limited. This drives people to look for better prospects in more politically stable and economically prosperous countries.

Example: In parts of West Africa, endemic corruption and weak governance have stifled economic growth, leading to high rates of youth migration. Many migrants embark on perilous journeys across the Sahara Desert and the Mediterranean Sea, aiming to reach Europe in search of work.

Characteristics of Economic Refugees

Economic refugees differ from traditional refugees in several key ways. Understanding these differences is important for developing tailored policy responses and for accurately identifying individuals' motivations for migration.

1. **Economic Motivations Rather Than Political Persecution**

   Unlike traditional refugees, economic refugees are not fleeing imminent threats to their lives, such as persecution, violence, or war. Instead, they are motivated primarily by the pursuit of economic opportunities. Their migration is often a calculated decision made in response to chronic poverty, unemployment, or the desire for a better standard of living.

2. **High Levels of Risk Tolerance**

   Economic refugees often display a high tolerance for risk, willing to undertake dangerous journeys and endure precarious conditions in the hope of securing better economic prospects. This willingness to take risks reflects the severe economic desperation they face in their home countries.

   Example: Economic migrants from Central America frequently travel through Mexico to reach the United States, facing dangers such as violence from criminal gangs, harsh environmental conditions, and the threat of exploitation by human traffickers. Despite these risks, many continue to make the journey in search of employment.

3. Remittances as a Key Motivation

For many economic refugees, the primary goal of migration is to secure employment that allows them to send remittances back to their families. Remittances play a vital role in supporting household incomes, funding education, and providing a safety net for relatives left behind.

Example: In the Philippines, millions of overseas workers send billions of dollars in remittances back home each year. These funds are crucial for the country's economy, supporting household consumption and alleviating poverty in rural areas.

Challenges in Identifying Economic Refugees

Distinguishing economic refugees from traditional refugees poses significant challenges for immigration authorities and policymakers. The line between economic hardship and persecution is often blurred, making it difficult to categorize migrants accurately.

1. Difficulty in Proving Economic Hardship

Unlike political persecution, which can sometimes be documented through reports of violence or government actions, economic hardship is harder to prove. Economic migrants may lack evidence of their circumstances, making it challenging for immigration officials to assess the validity of their claims.

2. Overlap with Traditional Refugee Claims

Many migrants present mixed motives, citing both economic hardship and political instability as reasons for their migration. This overlap complicates the process of determining eligibility for asylum or refugee status.

Example: Migrants from conflict-affected regions like Afghanistan or Venezuela may cite both economic collapse and threats of violence when seeking asylum, making it difficult for authorities to separate the economic aspects from genuine fears of persecution.

3. Policy Ambiguities and Inconsistent Definitions

International law does not provide a clear definition for economic refugees, and immigration policies vary widely between countries. This inconsistency creates confusion and leaves room for different interpretations, complicating the decision-making process for asylum officers and judges.

Implications for Host Countries

The arrival of economic refugees has significant social, economic, and political implications for host countries. While economic migrants can contribute to the labor market, they may also strain public services and fuel anti-immigrant sentiment.

1. **Economic Contributions and Labor Market Integration**

Economic migrants often take on low-skilled jobs that are vital to certain industries, such as agriculture, construction, and caregiving. Their labor can help fill gaps in the workforce, support economic growth, and contribute to the tax base.

2. **Strain on Public Services and Social Tensions**

The influx of economic refugees can place pressure on housing, healthcare, and social services, particularly in countries with limited resources. This strain can lead to social tensions, particularly in communities that already face high unemployment or economic challenges.

3. **Impact on Public Perception and Policy Debates**

The presence of economic refugees often shapes public perception of immigration policies, leading to debates about border control, eligibility for social benefits, and the broader impacts of migration on national identity.

Example: In several European countries, the arrival of large numbers of economic migrants has sparked public debates about the sustainability of the welfare state and has influenced the rise of political movements advocating for stricter immigration controls.

Conclusion

Economic migration is a natural consequence of global inequality, environmental changes, and economic opportunities in more developed nations. While economic refugees do not fit the traditional definition of refugees fleeing persecution, they represent a significant and growing portion of global migration flows. Addressing the challenges posed by economic migration requires a nuanced approach that recognizes the root causes of economic displacement while balancing the economic needs of host countries and the rights of migrants.

Moving forward, policymakers must develop targeted solutions that address the drivers of economic migration, enhance international cooperation, and create fair and sustainable immigration systems. By doing so, we can better manage the complexities of economic migration and ensure that immigration policies contribute to both national prosperity and global stability.

Chapter Twenty-Three: Challenges in Recognizing Economic Refugees

This chapter explores the complex task of identifying and recognizing economic refugees within existing immigration frameworks. Economic refugees are individuals driven to leave their home countries due to severe economic hardships rather than fleeing direct persecution or conflict. The absence of a clear legal definition for economic refugees complicates the process of distinguishing them from other categories of migrants, such as asylum seekers or labor migrants. We will examine the unique challenges faced by immigration authorities in determining the eligibility of economic refugees, the legal and policy gaps that exist, and the ethical dilemmas involved in addressing their needs. The chapter also discusses international efforts to adapt migration policies to account for economic displacement and considers the broader implications of failing to recognize economic refugees in a fair and consistent manner.

Introduction

Economic refugees occupy a grey area in global migration systems. Unlike traditional refugees, who flee their home countries due to persecution or armed conflict, economic refugees are driven primarily by the need to escape extreme poverty, unemployment, and other forms of economic distress. This group of migrants often lacks legal recognition under international refugee conventions, making it difficult for them to seek protection or legal status in host countries. The challenge lies in the fact that economic conditions can be life-threatening in their own way, pushing individuals to undertake perilous journeys in search of safety and better opportunities.

The international community has yet to agree on a framework for addressing the specific needs of economic refugees. While there are protections in place for asylum seekers fleeing violence, the plight of those escaping dire economic conditions often falls outside the scope of traditional refugee protections. As a result, economic refugees face numerous hurdles, including lengthy and uncertain legal processes, limited access to humanitarian aid, and the risk of deportation.

This chapter aims to shed light on the unique challenges in recognizing economic refugees, exploring the legal, policy, and ethical dimensions of this issue. We will discuss the difficulties faced by immigration authorities in assessing economic claims, the role of international law, and the need for new policy approaches to address this growing and overlooked group of migrants.

Legal and Policy Gaps in Recognizing Economic Refugees

The lack of a clear legal definition for economic refugees is one of the main obstacles to their recognition. International refugee law, as defined by the 1951 Refugee Convention and its 1967 Protocol, focuses on protecting individuals fleeing persecution based on race, religion, nationality, political opinion, or membership in a particular social group. Economic hardship is not included in this definition, leaving economic refugees without a legal basis for claiming asylum or protection.

1. **Absence of Legal Protections**

The 1951 Refugee Convention does not consider economic factors as valid grounds for refugee status, creating a legal void for individuals who are displaced primarily due to economic reasons. Without this recognition, economic refugees are often categorized as irregular migrants, making them vulnerable to detention, deportation, and limited access to basic services.

Example: In many Western countries, immigration authorities must evaluate whether an applicant's claim of economic hardship constitutes grounds for protection. However, because economic conditions are not seen as a legitimate basis for asylum, these claims are typically rejected, even when the applicant faces severe poverty or economic collapse in their home country.

2. Inconsistent National Policies

National immigration policies vary widely, with some countries adopting a more flexible approach to economic migration and others adhering strictly to the criteria set by international refugee law. This inconsistency creates disparities in how economic refugees are treated, depending on the host country's legal framework and political climate.

Example: In the European Union, economic migrants from Africa and the Middle East often face different treatment depending on the country in which they arrive. Some EU nations have implemented temporary protection measures for individuals fleeing economic collapse, while others focus solely on deportation, prioritizing the return of individuals who do not meet the traditional refugee criteria.

3. Lack of International Consensus

The international community has struggled to reach a consensus on how to address the issue of economic refugees. Efforts to expand the definition of a refugee to include those fleeing extreme economic hardship have been met with resistance from many countries, concerned that broadening the criteria could overwhelm their immigration systems and strain public resources.

Example: During global discussions on migration, such as the United Nations Global Compact for Safe, Orderly, and Regular Migration, member states debated whether to include provisions for economic refugees. While some nations advocated for greater recognition of economic displacement, others argued that it would dilute the protections afforded to traditional refugees and lead to an unmanageable increase in migration flows.

Challenges in Assessing Economic Hardship

Determining whether an individual qualifies as an economic refugee is inherently challenging, as economic conditions can vary widely even within the same country. Immigration authorities must consider multiple factors when evaluating claims of economic hardship, including the applicant's personal circumstances, the economic situation in their home country, and broader geopolitical dynamics.

1. Difficulty in Proving Economic Hardship

Unlike cases of political persecution, which can sometimes be documented through government records or witness testimony, economic hardship is often more subjective and difficult to prove. Applicants may lack the necessary documentation, such as employment records or financial statements, to demonstrate the severity of their situation.

Example: In regions affected by economic collapse, such as parts of Latin America, applicants may struggle to provide evidence of their economic distress. Hyperinflation, loss of employment, and widespread poverty are often cited as reasons for migration, but these factors are difficult to quantify in the context of asylum applications.

2. Overlapping Motivations for Migration

Many migrants cite both economic and non-economic reasons for leaving their home countries, making it challenging to categorize their claims. For instance, individuals from conflict-affected regions may be fleeing both violence and economic collapse, blurring the lines between economic refugees and traditional refugees.

Example: Migrants from countries experiencing prolonged conflict, such as certain Middle Eastern nations, often describe a combination of factors driving their decision to leave, including economic instability, food shortages, and ongoing violence. This overlap complicates the assessment process for immigration officials, who must determine the primary motive behind the migration.

3. Bias and Inconsistent Decision-Making

The lack of clear guidelines for assessing economic refugee claims can lead to inconsistent decision-making, influenced by biases or political considerations. Immigration officers may be more likely to reject economic claims, viewing them as less legitimate than claims of persecution, even when the economic conditions in the applicant's home country are dire.

Example: In many Western countries, asylum officers receive limited training on how to evaluate economic claims, often defaulting to the criteria set for traditional refugees. This can result in a higher rate of rejections for economic migrants, who may be forced to appeal or face immediate deportation.

The Ethical Dilemma of Economic Displacement

The exclusion of economic refugees from legal protections raises significant ethical questions. Economic hardship can be as life-threatening as persecution, particularly in cases of extreme poverty, food insecurity, or environmental degradation. By denying these individuals the right to seek asylum, the international community may be overlooking a key aspect of human suffering.

1. Economic Inequality and Moral Responsibility

The vast economic disparities between nations create a moral imperative for wealthier countries to consider the needs of economic refugees. While these individuals may not fit the traditional definition of refugees, they are often fleeing circumstances that threaten their basic human rights and dignity.

Recommendation: Develop a new legal category for economic refugees, providing temporary protection and access to humanitarian aid for individuals fleeing severe economic hardship. This could be similar to the Temporary Protected Status (TPS) used in the United States for individuals from countries experiencing environmental disasters or extreme instability.

2. The Risk of Creating a "Hierarchy of Deservingness"

The distinction between economic refugees and traditional refugees can create a hierarchy of deservingness, where those fleeing persecution are seen as more deserving of protection than those fleeing poverty. This distinction may fail to account for the fact that economic conditions, particularly in the context of climate change and systemic inequality, can be equally life-threatening.

Example: In global refugee forums, there is often a reluctance to equate economic hardship with persecution. However, as climate-induced migration increases, the line between economic and humanitarian displacement is becoming increasingly blurred, prompting calls for a more inclusive approach.

Moving Toward a More Inclusive Framework

To address the challenges of recognizing economic refugees, the international community must consider reforms that expand the scope of protection while balancing concerns about immigration control and resource allocation.

1. **Adopting a New International Protocol**

   Introduce an international protocol that recognizes economic displacement as a legitimate ground for temporary protection. This framework could be modeled on existing temporary protection measures, offering a pathway for economic refugees to receive humanitarian aid and temporary residency while their situation is assessed.

2. **Enhancing Regional Cooperation**

   Regional agreements could help manage economic migration by facilitating labor mobility and providing legal pathways for economic refugees. By working together, countries can reduce irregular migration and create opportunities for individuals to migrate legally for economic reasons.

   Example: In response to economic migration pressures, several Latin American countries have created regional frameworks to allow temporary labor migration, providing legal avenues for individuals seeking work without resorting to dangerous and irregular journeys.

Conclusion

The recognition of economic refugees remains a complex and contentious issue in global migration policy. While economic factors are not traditionally included in the definition of a refugee, they are increasingly driving migration flows, challenging the capacity of existing frameworks to respond. A more inclusive approach, which acknowledges the realities of economic displacement, is essential for addressing the needs of this vulnerable population.

Moving forward, policymakers must work to develop legal mechanisms, improve regional cooperation, and address the root causes of economic migration. By doing so, we can create a fairer, more compassionate immigration system that respects the dignity of all individuals seeking a better life, regardless of the reasons behind their displacement.

Chapter Twenty-Four: Routes Taken by Economic Refugees

This chapter explores the various routes taken by economic refugees as they navigate dangerous and often life-threatening journeys in pursuit of better economic opportunities. Economic refugees, unlike traditional asylum seekers, migrate primarily due to extreme poverty, environmental hardship, or the lack of basic living standards in their home countries. As a result, they are often left with no option but to resort to irregular migration routes. This chapter provides a comprehensive look at these diverse migration routes, including land, sea, and air, detailing the inherent dangers, the reliance on smuggling networks, and the social and political complexities that shape these journeys. Additionally, we will explore real-world examples of key migratory routes and analyze the broader implications of these migration flows for both host and transit countries.

Introduction

The journey of an economic refugee is typically shaped by desperation, uncertainty, and a dire need to improve life circumstances. Unlike asylum seekers fleeing immediate persecution, economic refugees are motivated by long-term deprivation and chronic hardship. Due to the lack of legal migration channels, their journeys are fraught with danger and risks, involving treacherous routes across land, sea, or air, and often subjecting them to the exploitation of smugglers and traffickers. This chapter will examine the major routes taken by economic refugees, the significant challenges they face, and the impact of their migration on host and transit countries.

Land Routes: The Overland Journey

Many economic refugees rely on land routes to reach wealthier or more stable neighboring countries. These journeys typically involve crossing borders on foot, by bus, or in the back of trucks, requiring them to traverse dangerous terrains like deserts, jungles, or conflict-affected areas. Migrants face numerous challenges, including evading border patrols, enduring harsh conditions, and dealing with smugglers.

1. Crossing Borders in Africa

In Africa, economic refugees often move within the region to find better opportunities. Sub-Saharan Africa is marked by widespread poverty and frequent armed conflicts, which lead people to migrate within the continent. For instance, refugees fleeing Niger, Chad, or South Sudan often journey across harsh environments to reach countries like Nigeria, Kenya, or South Africa, where there are better economic opportunities.

Example: Economic migrants from the Horn of Africa, including Ethiopia, Eritrea, and Somalia, often make their way to Sudan, hoping to eventually cross into North Africa and Europe. These overland journeys are grueling, requiring migrants to cross desert regions with limited access to water and food, while facing threats from militias, traffickers, and corrupt border guards. Many endure extreme heat, dehydration, and exhaustion, and those who cannot keep up are sometimes abandoned by smugglers.

2. The Trek from Central America to the United States

In Central America, one of the most notorious land routes is the journey northward to the United States. Migrants from Guatemala, Honduras, and El Salvador attempt to migrate via Mexico, facing a multitude of dangers such as deserts, jungles, rivers, and violent gangs. The journey often takes weeks or even months, and migrants must navigate treacherous landscapes while facing the threat of robbery, extortion, and violence.

Example: Migrants often join large caravans for safety, traveling on foot or using informal transportation, such as buses or cargo trains. Migrants riding "La Bestia" (The Beast), a network of freight trains, risk injury or death from falling off the moving train or being attacked by gangs who control sections of the route. Despite the dangers, many continue the journey driven by the hope of reaching the United States and finding stable work. The caravans also face frequent clashes with law enforcement, both in Mexico and at the U.S. border, adding another layer of danger to their journey.

3. The Balkan Route into Europe

Economic refugees from South Asia, the Middle East, and North Africa attempt to reach Europe through the Balkan route. This journey takes migrants through countries like Turkey, Greece, and Serbia, involving numerous border crossings and often requiring them to pass through areas with hostile environments and heavy law enforcement presence.

Example: Migrants entering Greece from Turkey continue their journey northward through the Balkans, navigating mountainous terrain and facing potential arrest. Many rely on smugglers to guide them through unfamiliar territory, paying significant sums for guidance and transportation. Despite the danger, the Balkan route remains a significant corridor for those seeking better opportunities in Europe. Migrants often face harsh weather, violence from border guards, and exploitation by smugglers, who may abandon them at critical points along the journey.

Sea Routes: Treacherous Crossings Over Water

Sea routes are often utilized when land routes are inaccessible. However, crossing vast bodies of water presents significant risks, including drowning, interception by coast guards, and exploitation by human traffickers. Many economic refugees embark on sea journeys in overcrowded, unsafe vessels that are prone to capsizing.

1. Crossing the Mediterranean to Europe

One of the most perilous sea routes is the Mediterranean crossing. Refugees from North Africa—primarily from Libya, Tunisia, or Algeria—board overcrowded boats operated by smugglers, which are often prone to capsizing due to poor conditions and overloading. The journey across the Mediterranean has become a symbol of the desperation faced by migrants seeking a better life in Europe.

Example: Migrants departing from Libya pay large sums to smugglers, traveling in inflatable rubber dinghies with dozens of others. The journey is dangerous, with migrants frequently relying on NGOs for rescue once they reach international waters. Many face dehydration, hypothermia, and the constant threat of drowning. Those who are intercepted by the Libyan Coast Guard are often returned to detention centers, where they face overcrowding, abuse, and a lack of basic necessities.

2. The Bay of Bengal and the Indian Ocean

Economic refugees from countries like Bangladesh or Myanmar often embark on dangerous sea journeys across the Bay of Bengal or the Indian Ocean to reach Malaysia, Indonesia, or Thailand. These routes are notoriously dangerous, with migrants facing harsh weather conditions, unseaworthy vessels, and the threat of human traffickers.

Example: Migrants from Myanmar, particularly the Rohingya minority, often make the journey to Malaysia in overcrowded wooden boats. The journey is risky, with threats from traffickers, abandonment, or detention. Many migrants spend weeks at sea without adequate food or water, and those who are intercepted by authorities are often detained in poor conditions or sent back to their country of origin.

Air Routes: High Cost and Complex Smuggling Networks

Air routes are less common due to the high costs involved. Those who choose air travel often rely on forged documents or smuggling networks. Air travel provides a faster route to destination countries, but the financial and legal risks are significant.

1. Use of Forged Documents

Air travel requires visas and travel documents, which many economic refugees cannot obtain. As a result, some turn to smuggling networks for forged passports and visas. The use of forged documents is risky, as it often results in arrest, detention, or deportation if discovered by authorities.

Example: Migrants from West Africa use forged passports to fly to European countries. Upon arrival, they face arrest or deportation if their documents are discovered to be fake, and they are often left in debt to smugglers. The use of false documents also makes it difficult for migrants to access legal protection or support services, leaving them vulnerable to exploitation.

2. Transit Through Multiple Countries

Some economic refugees travel through multiple countries to obscure their original point of departure. Smugglers often arrange for migrants to transit through countries with lenient visa requirements, allowing them to board flights to their final destination without raising suspicion.

Example: Migrants from South Asia may travel to a Gulf state before attempting to reach Europe or North America. Many are exploited during their time in transit, forced to work in harsh conditions or detained by local authorities. The lack of legal status in transit countries leaves them vulnerable to abuse, and they often face challenges in continuing their journey due to financial or legal barriers.

The Role of Smugglers and Traffickers

Smugglers and traffickers play a significant role in the journey of economic refugees, providing essential services while also exploiting them. Smuggling networks often operate with little regard for the safety or well-being of the migrants, focusing solely on profit.

1. Reliance on Smuggling Networks

Economic refugees unable to secure visas or travel permits often turn to smugglers for transport and guidance. Smugglers provide transportation, forged documents, and information about the safest routes, but they often exploit migrants by charging exorbitant fees and providing substandard services.

Example: Migrants from West Africa pay smugglers to cross the Sahara, through Libya, and across the Mediterranean. Smugglers often charge additional "fees" along the way, holding migrants hostage until payment is made. Many migrants are subjected to physical abuse, extortion, and even forced labor as they attempt to pay off their debts to smugglers.

2. Human Trafficking and Forced Labor

Many economic refugees fall victim to human trafficking, especially women and children, who may be forced into sex work or unpaid labor. Traffickers often lure migrants with false promises of safe passage or employment, only to exploit them once they are en route or upon arrival.

Example: Migrants from Southeast Asia traveling to Thailand or Malaysia are often trafficked into forced labor in the fishing industry or sweatshops, trapped by their debts. Women and children are particularly vulnerable, with many being forced into sex work or domestic servitude. The lack of legal protection and fear of deportation prevent many victims from seeking help, leaving them trapped in exploitative situations.

Challenges Faced by Economic Refugees During Transit

The journey of an economic refugee is marked by immense physical, emotional, and legal challenges. These challenges often continue even after reaching the intended destination, as migrants struggle to establish themselves in a new country.

1. Physical Hardship and Risk of Death

Economic refugees face severe physical challenges, including dehydration, malnutrition, and exposure to harsh environments. Many embark on journeys without adequate supplies, relying on smugglers who often fail to provide basic necessities.

Example: Migrants crossing the Sahara Desert suffer from dehydration and exposure, with many dying along the way. The desert's harsh conditions, including extreme temperatures and lack of water, make it one of the deadliest parts of the journey for migrants attempting to reach North Africa.

2. Emotional and Psychological Trauma

The journey of an economic refugee is not only physically exhausting but also emotionally and psychologically draining. Migrants face uncertainty, fear of arrest, and separation from family members, all of which contribute to significant mental health challenges.

Example: Migrants traveling in caravans from Central America to the United States often face prolonged periods of uncertainty, fearing deportation or violence from gangs. Many suffer from anxiety, depression, and post-traumatic stress due to the trauma experienced during their journey, including witnessing violence or experiencing abuse at the hands of smugglers or law enforcement.

3. Legal and Political Obstacles

Economic refugees face legal challenges as destination and transit countries often have restrictive immigration policies designed to deter irregular migration. Migrants are frequently detained, deported, or subjected to lengthy asylum processes, leaving them in a state of limbo.

Example: Migrants who enter Europe through Greece or Italy often face detention or deportation, as European countries have introduced increasingly strict policies to curb irregular migration. Many economic refugees are held in overcrowded detention centers, where they have limited access to legal representation or support services, and they may spend months or even years awaiting a decision on their asylum claims.

Conclusion

The routes taken by economic refugees—whether by land, sea, or air—are fraught with significant dangers, hardships, and uncertainties. Their journeys reflect the determination of those seeking a better future, even in the face of immense challenges. These routes are shaped by geography, political borders, and restrictive immigration policies, highlighting the urgent need for comprehensive and humane migration policies that provide safe and legal avenues for economic migration. Until such policies are developed, economic refugees will continue to embark on perilous journeys, driven by the hope of escaping poverty and achieving a better life.

The plight of economic refugees underscores the need for international cooperation and policy reform to address the root causes of economic migration, provide legal migration opportunities, and protect vulnerable individuals from exploitation. By understanding the challenges faced by economic refugees and the dangers inherent in their journeys, we can work towards creating a more equitable and humane global migration system that offers safety and opportunity for all. The goal must be to ensure that economic migration is no longer a journey of desperation but one of hope and opportunity.

Chapter Twenty-Five: Impacts on Asylum Systems and Social Services

This chapter examines the profound impacts of economic refugees on asylum systems and social services in destination countries. While economic refugees pursue better opportunities and escape poverty, their arrival—often through irregular channels—places significant strain on asylum systems that are already challenged by political refugees, as well as on the social services provided by host countries. This chapter discusses how asylum systems are affected by the growing number of applications, the complexities of distinguishing between political and economic migrants, and the challenges in maintaining fairness. Furthermore, we explore the pressures placed on healthcare, education, housing, and welfare services, and the implications for both migrants and host communities. Real-world examples provide insight into the multifaceted consequences of economic refugee flows.

Introduction

Economic refugees are often motivated by chronic poverty, lack of opportunities, and systemic economic failures in their home countries. Unlike traditional asylum seekers fleeing persecution, economic refugees are driven by economic hardships that have rendered their lives unsustainable. As such, their arrival in host countries presents a complex challenge—one that significantly impacts asylum systems and stretches social services to their limits.

The increasing influx of economic refugees complicates the asylum process, as officials are tasked with differentiating between genuine asylum seekers fleeing persecution and those escaping poverty. The blending of these two groups contributes to an overwhelming volume of asylum applications, which strains administrative resources and creates longer processing times. Meanwhile, the need to provide essential services to new arrivals, such as healthcare, housing, education, and social assistance, places a burden on public resources. This chapter delves into these impacts, focusing on the challenges faced by asylum systems, the pressure on social services, and the broader social and economic consequences for host countries and communities.

Impact on Asylum Systems

Economic refugees have a significant impact on asylum systems that were primarily designed to offer protection to those fleeing persecution. Asylum systems are often the first point of entry for migrants, regardless of whether they are seeking refuge from conflict or economic hardship. This influx has several consequences for the asylum system, creating procedural challenges, delaying decisions, and influencing public perception and policy.

1. **Increased Volume of Applications and Overburdened Systems**

   One of the most notable impacts of economic refugees on asylum systems is the increased volume of applications. As more individuals seeking economic relief enter asylum channels, authorities face an overwhelming number of claims, which slows down processing times for all applicants. The backlog of cases means that genuine asylum seekers face lengthy waits, during which their legal status remains in limbo. This can lead to years of uncertainty and delays in accessing rights, such as employment and education.

- *Example:* In Europe, the arrival of refugees from conflict zones like Syria was quickly followed by an influx of economic refugees from North and Sub-Saharan Africa. Many economic migrants lodged asylum claims upon arrival, contributing to a backlog of applications in countries like Germany and Italy. Asylum offices were flooded, with some cases taking two to three years to process, leaving individuals in a state of uncertainty.

2. **Difficulty Differentiating Between Economic Refugees and Genuine Asylum Seekers**

Another challenge presented by economic refugees is the difficulty of determining the legitimacy of their claims. While many economic refugees present credible narratives of hardship, they do not meet the criteria for refugee status as defined by international law. Asylum officers face the daunting task of distinguishing between applicants facing persecution and those seeking economic opportunities, often based on limited information and unreliable documentation.

- *Example:* In North America, asylum officers have struggled to differentiate between applicants from Central America fleeing generalized violence and those primarily motivated by economic hardship. Migrants from countries like Honduras and El Salvador may face extreme poverty alongside gang violence, blurring the lines between economic migration and asylum. This complexity leads to inconsistent decision-making and challenges the fairness of the asylum process.

3. Strain on Administrative Resources

The overwhelming number of asylum claims often leads to a strain on administrative resources. Governments must allocate additional funding to expand asylum processing capabilities, hire more officers, and manage growing caseloads. In many cases, funding is inadequate, which contributes to longer wait times and compromises the quality of decision-making.

- *Example:* The asylum system in Greece faced collapse under the pressure of applications from both political refugees fleeing the Syrian civil war and economic migrants from Africa and South Asia. Limited staffing and resources left asylum seekers waiting in camps with inadequate services, and the quality of decisions suffered as overwhelmed officers attempted to process applications quickly.

4. Undermining the Integrity of the Asylum System

The influx of economic refugees into asylum channels can also undermine the integrity of the asylum system. When economic migrants lodge asylum claims, it creates a perception that the asylum system is being abused, which can erode public trust and support. This erosion of trust can lead to calls for stricter asylum policies and an increased focus on deterrence rather than protection, ultimately jeopardizing the rights of genuine refugees.

- *Example:* In the United States, the perception that economic migrants are abusing the asylum system has led to policy changes aimed at restricting access to asylum, including limits on asylum claims at the southern border. These measures often prioritize deterrence over due process, making it more difficult for genuine asylum seekers to access the protection they need.

Impact on Social Services

The arrival of economic refugees also places significant pressure on the social services available in host countries. Social services—including healthcare, education, housing, and welfare—are already strained in many countries, and the arrival of a large number of refugees can exacerbate these pressures, creating competition for limited resources.

1. **Healthcare Systems Under Strain**

   The increased demand for healthcare services is one of the most immediate impacts of the arrival of economic refugees. Many refugees arrive with untreated medical conditions, including communicable diseases, injuries sustained during their journey, or chronic health issues resulting from years of poverty. Healthcare systems in host countries must accommodate this increased demand, which often leads to longer wait times, overburdened hospitals, and increased costs.

- *Example:* In Italy, where many economic refugees arrive by boat across the Mediterranean, hospitals in coastal cities have reported a significant increase in patient load. Many arrivals require urgent medical care upon arrival, including treatment for dehydration, malnutrition, and injuries. This additional demand places a strain on healthcare workers and stretches resources thin, impacting the quality of care available to the general population.

2. **Pressure on Housing and Shelter Systems**

Housing is another area where the impact of economic refugees is deeply felt. Host countries must find housing for newly arrived refugees, often in a context of limited affordable housing stock. The influx of economic refugees exacerbates the housing shortage, leading to competition for affordable accommodation. This can drive up rental prices and create tension between refugees and local populations who are also struggling to find affordable housing.

- *Example:* In Germany, the arrival of hundreds of thousands of refugees between 2015 and 2016—including both political and economic migrants—led to a housing crisis in many cities. Refugees were housed in temporary accommodations, including gyms and converted office spaces, while authorities scrambled to provide permanent housing. The increased demand drove up rental prices, particularly in urban areas, creating resentment among local residents who faced increased competition for affordable housing.

3. Education Systems Facing Challenges

The education system in host countries must also adapt to accommodate the needs of refugee children. Economic refugee families often arrive with children who need to be integrated into local schools. Schools must address language barriers, gaps in formal education, and the trauma many refugee children have experienced. The increased demand for educational services can strain resources, particularly in schools that are already struggling with overcrowding and limited funding.

- *Example:* In France, schools in urban areas with large refugee populations have reported challenges in integrating refugee children. Teachers face difficulties managing classrooms with diverse linguistic and cultural needs, and the lack of adequate support staff further complicates the situation. The pressure on the education system has led to concerns about the quality of education provided to both refugee children and local students.

4. **Social Welfare and Public Assistance Programs**

Economic refugees often rely on social welfare programs upon arrival, as they may not have the means to support themselves. Access to public assistance, such as unemployment benefits, housing subsidies, and food aid, is crucial for their survival. However, the increased demand for welfare services can strain public finances, particularly in countries with already stretched social safety nets. The perception that refugees are a drain on public resources can also lead to resentment and hostility from host communities.

- *Example:* In the United Kingdom, the arrival of economic refugees has led to increased competition for welfare benefits, particularly housing subsidies. Many refugees are unable to find employment immediately due to language barriers or lack of recognition of their qualifications, leaving them reliant on public assistance. This increased demand has led to public criticism and calls for stricter eligibility requirements for welfare benefits.

Social and Economic Consequences for Host Communities

The arrival of economic refugees also has broader social and economic consequences for host communities. While refugees can contribute positively to the economy in the long term, their initial arrival can create challenges that need to be managed effectively to ensure positive outcomes for both refugees and host communities.

1. **Competition for Low-Skilled Jobs**

Economic refugees, particularly those who enter the country through irregular channels, often find themselves working in low-skilled jobs, sometimes in the informal sector. Their willingness to work for lower wages can create competition for jobs, particularly in industries such as agriculture, construction, and service. This competition can lead to tensions with local workers, who may feel that their opportunities are being undermined.

- *Example:* In Southern Spain, the arrival of economic refugees from Africa has led to increased competition for agricultural jobs in the region's vast fruit and vegetable farms. Migrants often work for lower wages, leading to resentment among local laborers who feel their livelihoods are threatened. This competition has contributed to tensions between migrants and local communities, with incidents of discrimination and hostility reported.

2. **Impact on Social Cohesion and Community Relations**

The presence of economic refugees can also impact social cohesion in host communities. When local residents perceive refugees as a burden on public resources or as competitors for jobs and housing, it can lead to resentment and hostility. In some cases, this has resulted in social tensions, protests, or even violence against refugee populations.

- *Example:* In some parts of Greece, local communities have protested the establishment of refugee reception centers, citing concerns about the impact on local resources and security. The influx of refugees, including economic migrants, has strained local services and contributed to a sense of resentment among residents, leading to protests and community divisions.

3. **Positive Contributions Over Time**

Despite the challenges, economic refugees can make positive contributions to host communities over time. Many refugees are eager to work, start businesses, and contribute to the economy. Given the right support—such as access to language classes, vocational training, and pathways to legal employment—economic refugees can help address labor shortages, revitalize communities, and contribute to economic growth.

- *Example:* In Canada, refugees have been able to contribute positively to the economy by filling labor shortages in industries such as manufacturing and agriculture. Programs that provide language training and support for credential recognition have helped refugees integrate into the workforce, allowing them to become self-sufficient and contribute to their new communities.

Conclusion

The impact of economic refugees on asylum systems and social services in host countries is complex and multifaceted. The increased volume of asylum applications places a strain on processing systems, delays decisions, and undermines the integrity of the asylum system. Meanwhile, the demand for social services, including healthcare, housing, education, and welfare, creates challenges for host countries that must balance their obligations to refugees with the needs of their citizens.

Addressing these challenges requires a nuanced approach that recognizes the rights and needs of economic refugees while ensuring that host communities are not overwhelmed. This includes investing in social services, improving asylum processing efficiency, and developing policies that support the integration of refugees into society. With the right measures in place, economic refugees can transition from being perceived as a burden to becoming contributors to their host communities, benefiting both themselves and the societies they join.

Chapter Twenty-Six: Policy Solutions and Alternatives

This chapter examines policy solutions and alternatives that host countries can implement to address the challenges posed by economic refugees and irregular migration. The goal is to find approaches that balance humanitarian obligations, economic interests, and security concerns. We explore current policy frameworks, innovative pilot projects, and successful international practices that have been implemented to improve migration management. This chapter also examines the role of international cooperation, labor migration programs, and development initiatives aimed at reducing the root causes of economic migration. Through an extensive discussion of these approaches, we aim to provide comprehensive solutions for a complex global issue.

Introduction

The movement of economic refugees, particularly through irregular migration channels, presents a major challenge for countries that are grappling with competing priorities—upholding humanitarian principles, protecting national security, and managing limited resources. Traditional asylum systems were designed to address political persecution, not the economic desperation that drives millions to seek a better life. As a result, policymakers must rethink their approach to managing economic migration and ensure that pathways for movement align with current global realities.

This chapter explores a wide range of policy solutions and alternatives aimed at managing economic migration and supporting both host and origin countries. We examine reforms to asylum systems, labor migration pathways, cooperation between countries of origin and host countries, and development-focused solutions aimed at addressing the root causes of migration. We also explore the challenges inherent in balancing border control with humanitarian values. In doing so, we aim to provide a roadmap for governments, international organizations, and stakeholders working to build a more effective and equitable global migration system.

Reforming Asylum Systems to Address Economic Migration

Asylum systems were created to provide protection to individuals fleeing persecution. However, economic migrants often use these systems as a last resort to escape poverty and find better opportunities. To better manage the influx of economic refugees, reforms to asylum systems must be implemented to maintain their integrity while providing appropriate avenues for economic migrants.

1. **Streamlining and Expediting Asylum Processing**

   One of the key issues facing asylum systems today is the lengthy processing time that leaves applicants in limbo for years. By streamlining and expediting the processing of asylum claims, governments can reduce backlogs and ensure that only those with legitimate claims are granted refugee status. Implementing a fast-track system for applicants from low-risk countries could allow authorities to focus more resources on evaluating complex cases that require additional scrutiny.

- *Example:* Several countries, including Canada and Germany, have implemented fast-track processing systems that prioritize asylum claims based on the applicant's country of origin. This allows authorities to expedite cases from countries where the likelihood of genuine persecution is lower, freeing up resources to evaluate applications from high-risk areas where persecution is more prevalent.

2. Differentiating Between Economic Migrants and Refugees

Asylum systems should be reformed to clearly differentiate between economic migrants and genuine asylum seekers. Specialized screening tools and training for asylum officers can help distinguish between claims based on economic hardship and those rooted in persecution. Clear criteria and standards must be established to ensure that economic migrants are not misusing the asylum system, which is intended for those in genuine need of protection.

- *Example:* The European Union has developed a training module for asylum officers that emphasizes recognizing signs of economic migration versus political persecution. Officers receive additional training on assessing credibility and examining supporting evidence to make more accurate determinations.

3. Establishing Complementary Protection Programs

One alternative to the traditional asylum system is the establishment of complementary protection programs for individuals who do not qualify as refugees under the 1951 Refugee Convention but still face serious harm if returned to their home countries. These programs could provide temporary protection to economic migrants from regions affected by extreme poverty, environmental disasters, or conflict-induced instability.

- *Example:* Some European countries, such as Sweden, have introduced forms of complementary protection, offering temporary residency to individuals from conflict zones or regions experiencing severe humanitarian crises. These programs are intended to provide temporary support while conditions in the country of origin stabilize, allowing for safe return when feasible.

Expanding Legal Labor Migration Pathways

One of the most effective ways to manage economic migration is by expanding legal pathways for labor migration. By providing economic migrants with legal avenues to enter the workforce, host countries can reduce irregular migration, address labor shortages, and support economic growth.

1. **Seasonal and Sector-Specific Work Programs**

Seasonal work programs and sector-specific visas can provide legal pathways for economic migrants to work in sectors with labor shortages, such as agriculture, construction, and hospitality. These programs can be structured to allow migrants to return home after the completion of their work contracts, thus reducing the pressure on asylum systems and encouraging circular migration.

- *Example:* The United States' H-2A and H-2B visa programs allow agricultural and non-agricultural seasonal workers to legally work in the U.S. on a temporary basis. These programs have been successful in addressing labor shortages in industries that rely heavily on seasonal labor, while also providing economic opportunities for migrants.

2. **Bilateral Labor Migration Agreements**

Bilateral agreements between countries of origin and host countries can provide a framework for managed labor migration that benefits both parties. These agreements can include provisions for skill development, labor rights, and the return and reintegration of migrants after their work contracts are completed.

- *Example:* Spain has signed bilateral labor migration agreements with several countries in Latin America and North Africa. These agreements allow for the temporary migration of workers to fill labor shortages in agriculture and construction, while also ensuring that migrants receive training and support to reintegrate upon their return home.

3. **Pathways to Permanent Residency for Skilled Workers**

In addition to seasonal and temporary work visas, host countries should provide pathways to permanent residency for skilled workers who contribute to the economy. Creating incentives for skilled economic migrants to stay and invest in their host countries can promote integration and long-term economic growth.

- *Example:* Canada's Express Entry system allows skilled workers to apply for permanent residency based on their skills, education, and work experience. The program provides a legal pathway for economic migrants to contribute to the Canadian economy while offering the possibility of long-term integration.

Cooperation Between Host Countries and Countries of Origin

Addressing economic migration requires collaboration between host countries and countries of origin. By working together, countries can create conditions that reduce the need for irregular migration while promoting safe and orderly movement.

1. **Development Aid and Addressing Root Causes**

One of the most effective ways to reduce economic migration is to address the root causes that drive individuals to leave their home countries. Host countries can provide development aid, invest in infrastructure, and support economic initiatives in countries of origin to create opportunities and improve living conditions. Reducing poverty, improving education, and promoting political stability can mitigate the factors that drive migration.

- *Example:* The European Union's Partnership Framework on Migration aims to address the root causes of migration by providing development aid to countries in Africa. By investing in job creation, education, and infrastructure, the program seeks to reduce the push factors that lead to irregular migration.

2. **Reintegration Programs for Returnees**

Reintegration programs can support the return of economic migrants to their home countries by providing training, financial assistance, and job placement services. By ensuring that returnees have opportunities upon their return, host countries can reduce the likelihood of re-migration and help migrants reintegrate successfully.

- *Example:* Germany's "Returning to New Opportunities" program provides financial assistance, vocational training, and support for small business creation to individuals who voluntarily return to their home countries. The program aims to ensure that returnees have sustainable livelihoods and do not feel compelled to migrate again.

3. **Combating Human Trafficking and Smuggling Networks**

Cooperation between countries of origin and host countries is essential to combat human trafficking and smuggling networks that facilitate irregular migration. These networks exploit vulnerable individuals and contribute to the dangerous and often deadly journeys undertaken by economic migrants. By sharing intelligence, conducting joint operations, and targeting organized crime, countries can disrupt these networks and reduce irregular migration.

- *Example:* The United Nations Office on Drugs and Crime (UNODC) has facilitated cross-border cooperation between countries in North Africa and Europe to combat human trafficking and smuggling. Joint operations have resulted in the dismantling of several smuggling networks, improving security for migrants and reducing irregular migration flows.

Managing Irregular Migration and Ensuring Security

Managing economic migration also requires effective border management and security measures to prevent irregular migration while ensuring that those in genuine need of protection can access asylum.

1. **Border Management and Screening**

   Effective border management is essential to prevent irregular migration and ensure that individuals entering a country are properly screened. Border officials must be trained to identify vulnerable individuals, such as trafficking victims, while also preventing illegal entry. Investment in technology, such as biometric screening and surveillance, can enhance border management while ensuring security.

   - *Example:* Several European countries have implemented biometric screening at border crossings to identify individuals attempting to enter using false identities. This technology has been effective in preventing repeat entries by individuals who have previously been deported.

2. **Regularization Programs for Long-Term Irregular Migrants**

   Regularization programs can provide a solution for long-term irregular migrants who have integrated into host countries and contribute positively to society. By providing a legal status, these programs can help individuals access healthcare, education, and legal employment, reducing their vulnerability to exploitation.

- *Example:* In Italy, the government implemented a regularization program for undocumented migrants who were employed in essential sectors, such as agriculture and domestic work, during the COVID-19 pandemic. This program recognized the contributions of irregular migrants while providing them with legal status and access to social services.

3. **Safe and Legal Alternatives to Irregular Migration**

Creating safe and legal alternatives to irregular migration is essential to reduce the risks faced by economic migrants. Expanding family reunification pathways, providing humanitarian visas, and offering scholarships for students from developing countries are all ways to provide legal alternatives that reduce the need for irregular migration.

- *Example:* Portugal introduced a humanitarian visa for individuals from countries affected by environmental disasters and armed conflict. This visa allows applicants to enter Portugal legally and apply for asylum, providing a safe alternative to irregular migration and dangerous journeys.

Conclusion

The challenges presented by economic refugees and irregular migration require a comprehensive, multifaceted approach that balances humanitarian obligations with national security and economic interests. By reforming asylum systems, expanding legal labor migration pathways, enhancing cooperation between host countries and countries of origin, and managing borders effectively, policymakers can create a migration system that is fair, humane, and efficient.

Addressing the root causes of economic migration through development aid, investing in infrastructure, and promoting stability in countries of origin are essential components of a long-term solution. By creating opportunities and improving living conditions in migrants' home countries, the pressure on asylum systems and social services in host countries can be alleviated, leading to better outcomes for all involved.

Ultimately, a coordinated, international effort is required to manage economic migration in a way that benefits both migrants and host countries. Through thoughtful policy solutions and collaboration, the global community can create a migration system that upholds human dignity, supports economic development, and ensures security for all.

Part V: Author's Reflections and Recommendations

Chapter Twenty-Seven: The Author's Perspective: Cultural Integration, Religious Reformation, and Preserving Western Values

This chapter presents the author's perspective on the importance of cultural integration for immigrants and refugees, emphasizing the need to adapt to Western values and address challenges posed by extremist ideologies to protect democratic and secular foundations.

Introduction

As the Western world faces increasing challenges related to immigration and cultural diversity, it becomes vital to address the responsibilities that accompany the rights and freedoms offered to new arrivals. Immigrants and refugees must not only adapt to their new environment but also embrace the core values of their host countries. This chapter explores how cultural integration and religious reformation can help maintain the integrity of Western values, particularly in light of conservative religious ideologies that may clash with democratic and secular norms. It is a call for proactive efforts to safeguard the liberties that define Western civilization, while also ensuring that diverse communities can thrive without compromising fundamental human rights and social harmony.

Adapting to Western Values

The decision to move to a new country comes with immense opportunities but also substantial responsibilities. When refugees and immigrants arrive in Western countries, they often seek freedom, safety, and a better future. However, with these rights come obligations to respect and adapt to the values, norms, and traditions of the host country.

It is essential to acknowledge that while the Western world has largely embraced secularism, democracy, and individual freedoms, certain religious ideologies, particularly the conservative and extremist interpretations of Islam, have shown a distinct incompatibility with these values. If we are to preserve the democratic foundations, freedoms, and way of life that our ancestors fought so hard to build, it is crucial that we address this issue directly and without hypocrisy.

The Issue of Religious Incompatibility

Western nations are built on the principles of freedom of speech, gender equality, rule of law, and the separation of church and state. These values form the bedrock of Western societies, providing a framework that ensures human rights and individual freedoms for all citizens. However, many conservative interpretations of Islamic law (Shariah) are fundamentally at odds with these principles. For example, Shariah law does not recognize the equality of women and men, often prescribes harsh punishments for acts considered normal in Western societies, and restricts freedom of expression, especially when it comes to criticism of religion.

Historically, Western countries have adopted a pluralistic approach, allowing people of various religious backgrounds to live freely and practice their beliefs. However, this pluralism has been tested by the rise of religious fundamentalism, particularly Islamic extremism, which has not only rejected Western values but has actively sought to replace them.

The Urgent Need for Cultural Integration: Adapting to Western Values

In the modern era, migration to Western countries has been driven by a search for safety, freedom, and economic opportunity. Many refugees and immigrants fleeing conflict, persecution, or economic hardship arrive in the West hoping for a fresh start. However, with these opportunities comes a significant responsibility: the responsibility to integrate into the host country's culture, embrace its values, and respect its laws.

For too long, Western nations have prioritized accommodating cultural differences without adequately addressing the challenges posed by certain religious ideologies, particularly those rooted in conservative interpretations of Islam. It is time to confront this issue directly, for the sake of preserving the freedoms and democratic values that have defined Western civilization.

The Incompatibility of Conservative Islamic Ideologies with Western Values

Western countries are built on principles that uphold individual freedoms, gender equality, rule of law, and the separation of religion and state. These are not mere preferences; they are the foundations of democracy and human rights. In contrast, conservative interpretations of Islam often adhere to Shariah law, which fundamentally conflicts with Western legal and cultural norms. Under Shariah law, women are not equal to men, freedom of speech is restricted, apostasy can be punishable by death, and harsh corporal punishments are prescribed for offenses that are not considered crimes in the West.

The issue is not with Islam as a whole, but with its more rigid and fundamentalist interpretations that do not adapt to the democratic and secular frameworks of Western societies. The expectation that Western countries should alter their laws, accommodate conservative religious practices, and even suppress criticism of religion undermines the very freedoms that immigrants and refugees came to enjoy. If left unchecked, these demands risk reshaping the social and legal fabric of host nations.

A Call for Adaptation and Religious Reformation

It is time for Western countries to assert a clear expectation: immigrants and refugees must be willing to adapt to the values of the host country. This includes a willingness to abandon certain religious practices that are incompatible with the democratic and secular principles of the West. The notion that one should be free to practice their religion is respected, but it cannot extend to practices that violate the basic human rights and freedoms enshrined in Western laws.

This requirement should apply particularly to conservative interpretations of Islam that conflict with Western values. If a potential immigrant or refugee believes that the host country's laws are fundamentally flawed or contrary to their religious beliefs, they should present these claims in a court of law, using their own personal funds. However, even if such a challenge were successful, it should serve as grounds for disqualification from immigration, as it indicates an unwillingness to integrate into the cultural and legal norms of the host nation.

The Consequences of Failing to Act

The long-term implications of ignoring this issue are severe. As the Muslim population grows in Western countries, there is a real risk that Islam could become a dominant religion, with Shariah law becoming a significant force. This shift would have profound implications for future generations, jeopardizing the freedoms, rights, and democratic values that have been hard-won over centuries.

The possibility of a majority-Muslim population in Western countries could lead to increased political pressure for the implementation of laws that align with Islamic principles, potentially replacing the secular and inclusive legal systems currently in place. In countries where Islam has become the dominant religion, we have seen a push towards implementing Shariah law, which can lead to the erosion of rights for women, religious minorities, and LGBTQ+ individuals. The Western world must not ignore these examples or assume it is immune to similar changes. Without proactive measures, there is a genuine risk that the freedoms and democratic principles that define Western societies could be eroded.

Political Hypocrisy and the Need for Action

The reluctance of Western politicians to address the issue of religious incompatibility head-on is a form of hypocrisy that endangers the very foundations of our societies. Many political leaders, in their pursuit of appeasement and political correctness, have failed to recognize the dangers of allowing extremist ideologies to take root. This failure is not only shortsighted but also a betrayal of the values that our ancestors fought to protect.

It is time for politicians to take a stand. They must prioritize the preservation of Western values and democracy over the fear of offending religious sensibilities. This is not a call for religious persecution but rather a demand for cultural adaptation and integration. It is an acknowledgment that while diversity enriches societies, it cannot come at the cost of sacrificing fundamental freedoms and democratic principles.

A New Policy for Immigration and Refugee Acceptance

To prevent the gradual erosion of Western values, new policies must be put in place. One of the core requirements for immigrants and refugees should be a commitment to uphold and respect the values of the host country, including gender equality, freedom of speech, and the rule of law. Applicants should be required to demonstrate their willingness to adapt to these values before being granted entry.

Furthermore, Western countries must be vigilant against the spread of extremist ideologies. This includes monitoring religious organizations and educational institutions that promote views incompatible with democratic values. Governments should take strong action against hate speech and incitement to violence, regardless of the religious background of those involved.

Conclusion: Acting Before It's Too Late

The time to act is now, before it is too late. The West cannot afford to wait until its democratic values are at risk of being overridden by religious ideologies that reject the principles of freedom, equality, and secular governance. The future of Western civilization depends on our willingness to uphold these values and ensure that those who come to our shores share in this commitment.

We must move beyond political correctness and confront the realities of cultural and religious integration. This is not a matter of discrimination but of safeguarding the freedoms that define us. If we fail to act, we risk losing the very essence of what makes Western societies a beacon of hope for so many around the world.

It is time for politicians to put aside their hypocrisy, stop appeasing extremist ideologies, and start defending the values that make the West a place of freedom and opportunity. Only through firm and decisive action can we ensure a future where democracy, freedom, and human rights continue to flourish.

Appendices

The appendices of this book serve to provide readers with additional resources, contextual background, and supplementary information to enhance their understanding of the topics covered. By including the following sections, this appendix aims to deepen the reader's insights into the dynamics of immigration, cultural integration, national security, and the broader sociopolitical implications discussed throughout the book.

Appendix A: Glossary of Key Terms

The concepts addressed in this book span a wide range of fields—from legal definitions of refugee and asylum systems to socio-political terms related to cultural integration and national security. This glossary provides definitions of key terms used throughout the book, ensuring that readers of all backgrounds can follow the discussion without ambiguity. It includes terminology such as:

- **Asylum Seeker:** An individual seeking international protection whose request for refugee status has not yet been determined.

- **Catch and Release:** A practice in which individuals detained for entering a country illegally are released while awaiting an immigration hearing, rather than being detained throughout the process.

- **Cultural Integration:** The process by which immigrants adapt to the cultural norms, values, and social behaviors of the host country.

- **Economic Refugee:** A person who flees their country primarily due to economic hardship, poverty, or a lack of economic opportunities, rather than fear of persecution.

- **Espionage:** The act of spying or using spies, typically by governments, to obtain political or military information.

- **Extremism:** The holding of extreme political or religious views that can lead to actions in conflict with societal norms or established laws.

- **Fake Refugees:** Individuals who provide false information or misuse the asylum system to gain entry to a country without a genuine need for international protection.

- **Family Reunification:** An immigration policy that allows family members of immigrants already residing in a host country to join them.

- **Family Reunification Programs:** Immigration policies that allow family members to join their relatives who have settled legally in a host country.

- **Human Smuggling:** The facilitation of illegal entry of a person into a country where they are not authorized to enter, typically in exchange for financial or other benefits.

- **Human Trafficking:** The illegal trade of humans for the purposes of forced labor, sexual exploitation, or involuntary servitude.

- **Integration:** The process through which immigrants become part of their host society, involving adaptation to cultural values, norms, and laws.

- **Intifada:** Arabic for "uprising"; historically refers to two Palestinian uprisings against Israeli occupation but sometimes used in other contexts to denote rebellion or resistance.

- **Investment-Based Immigration:** A pathway to residency or citizenship offered to individuals who invest a significant sum of money in a host country's economy, often used to attract wealth.

- **IRGC (Islamic Revolutionary Guard Corps):** A branch of Iran's Armed Forces, often accused of supporting terrorist activities and engaging in clandestine operations abroad.

- **Islamic Extremism:** The ideology that promotes the establishment of a political system based on radical interpretations of Islamic law, often advocating for violence to achieve these goals.

- **Islamic Fundamentalism:** A movement advocating for a return to fundamentalist interpretations of Islam, often rejecting secularism and modernity.

- **LGBTQ Asylum Claim:** A claim for asylum based on persecution due to an individual's sexual orientation or gender identity.

- **LGBTQ Identity:** Refers to individuals who identify as Lesbian, Gay, Bisexual, Transgender, or Queer. In some cases, individuals falsely claim LGBTQ identity to seek asylum in countries that protect LGBTQ rights.

- **Legal Immigration Pathways:** Official means by which individuals can migrate to another country, typically involving processes such as family reunification, skilled worker visas, investment visas, or humanitarian programs.

- **Malicious Organizations:** Groups or networks that exploit legal immigration channels to achieve goals like espionage, financial crimes, or destabilization of societies.

- **Policy Reform:** Changes made to improve a policy, often to address identified issues or adapt to changing circumstances.

- **Political Asylum:** Protection given by a government to someone fleeing political persecution in their home country.

- **Refugee:** A person who has fled their country due to persecution, war, or violence and has been recognized as needing protection under international law.

- **Refugee Status:** The official recognition granted to individuals who meet the international definition of a refugee, typically by demonstrating a well-founded fear of persecution based on race, religion, nationality, membership in a particular social group, or political opinion.

- **Religious Reformation:** The process of changing or modifying certain religious practices or beliefs, particularly those that conflict with the democratic and secular principles of a society.

- **Secularism:** The principle of separation of government institutions and representatives from religious institutions and influences.

- **Shariah Law:** The Islamic legal system derived from the Quran and Hadith, governing aspects of a Muslim's personal and social life, often criticized for its incompatibility with Western principles of gender equality and freedom.

- **Smuggling Networks:** Organized groups that facilitate illegal crossings of borders in exchange for monetary compensation, often exploiting vulnerable individuals seeking a better future.

- **Western Values:** Cultural, political, and ethical beliefs that are often associated with Western countries, including freedom of speech, democracy, gender equality, individual rights, and the rule of law.

- **Xenophobia:** Dislike or prejudice against people from other countries, often resulting from the fear that immigrants will harm the host society's culture or economy.

Appendix B: Historical Context and Timelines

To better understand the modern challenges surrounding migration, integration, and religious extremism, it's important to look back at the events that shaped today's realities. This section offers a brief historical overview of:

1. **The Evolution of the Modern Refugee System**: A timeline tracing major international events that led to the development of the current asylum framework, including the establishment of the UN Refugee Convention in 1951 and subsequent amendments.

2. **Migration Patterns in the 21st Century**: A summary of major migratory waves since 2000, including conflicts in the Middle East, economic instability in Latin America, and the effects of climate change on migration.

3. **Rise of Extremist Movements**: A timeline highlighting significant events related to the rise of extremist ideologies, with a particular focus on the spread of radical Islamic groups and their influence on Western countries.

Appendix C: International Conventions, Laws, and Agreements

This section provides a summary of key international conventions and agreements that govern the movement of people across borders and the rights of migrants and refugees. These include:

- **The 1951 Refugee Convention and the 1967 Protocol**: Key international agreements defining refugee rights and state responsibilities.

- **Dublin Regulation**: A European Union regulation determining which EU member state is responsible for processing an asylum claim.

- **Global Compact on Refugees**: An international agreement aimed at improving the response to large movements of refugees and supporting host countries.

Appendix D: Notable Case Studies and Examples

Throughout the book, various case studies and real-life examples are referenced. This appendix provides detailed accounts of some of these cases, without using specific names or identifying information, to protect the privacy of individuals and institutions involved. Examples include:

- **Case Study: The Southern Border Crisis in the United States**: Detailed exploration of the challenges faced by migrants traveling through Central America and Mexico to reach the United States, including the tactics used by human smugglers.

- **Case Study: Iranian Agents in Canada**: An overview of documented incidents of foreign agents infiltrating Western countries through legal immigration channels, focusing on those with ties to the Islamic Republic of Iran.

- **Case Study: LGBTQ Asylum Fraud**: Examination of instances where individuals have falsely claimed LGBTQ identity to gain asylum status in Western countries, and the broader impact of such claims on genuine refugees.

Appendix E: Policy Proposals and Recommendations

This section consolidates the various policy suggestions presented throughout the book, offering a concise reference for policymakers, scholars, and readers interested in actionable reforms. Key proposals include:

1. **Enhanced Vetting for Immigration and Refugee Programs**: Measures to strengthen background checks and reduce fraudulent claims.

2. **Requirements for Cultural Integration**: Recommendations for mandatory integration programs, focusing on language skills, legal education, and the values of the host country.

3. **Monitoring and Regulation of Religious Institutions**: Suggestions for monitoring religious institutions that promote ideologies incompatible with democratic principles and human rights.

Sources / References

Below is a list of sources that informed the discussions and analyses throughout this book. These references provide additional information and context for readers interested in delving deeper into topics such as migration, cultural integration, and national security.

General Sources on Migration and Refugee Systems

1. **United Nations High Commissioner for Refugees (UNHCR)**

   - "Convention and Protocol Relating to the Status of Refugees." UNHCR, 1951.

     https://www.unhcr.org/1951-refugee-convention.html

2. **International Organization for Migration (IOM)**

   - "World Migration Report 2022." IOM, 2022.

     https://publications.iom.int/books/world-migration-report-2022

3. **European Commission - Migration and Home Affairs**

   - "Dublin Regulation." European Union, 2021.

     https://home-affairs.ec.europa.eu/policies/migration-and-asylum/common-european-asylum-system/country-responsible-asylum-application-dublin-regulation_en

Sources on Immigration Policies and Security Risks

4. **Brookings Institution**

   - Koser, Khalid. "When Refugees and Migrants Become a Security Issue." Brookings, 2015.

     https://www.brookings.edu/articles/when-is-migration-a-security-issue/

5. **Pew Research Center**

   - "Muslims in Western Europe: Attitudes and Trends." Pew Research Center, 2019.

     https://www.pewresearch.org/global/2019/10/14/minority-groups/

6. **RAND Corporation**

   - Jackson, Brian A. "The Terrorism Threat and U.S. Government Response: Operational and Organizational Factors." RAND Corporation, 2020.

Sources on Cultural Integration and Challenges

7. **Douglas Murray**

   - "The Strange Death of Europe: Immigration, Identity, Islam." Bloomsbury Continuum, 2017.

8. **Betts, Alexander, and Paul Collier**

   - "Refuge: Transforming a Broken Refugee System." Penguin Random House, 2018.

9. **Foreign Affairs**

   - "Europe's Migration Crisis: Lessons from the Past." Foreign Affairs, 2017.

Sources on Extremism and Security Risks

10. **Counter Extremism Project**

   - "Iran's Proxy Groups and Threats to Global Security." Counter Extremism Project, 2021.

11. **Global Terrorism Index**

   - "Global Terrorism Index 2023: Measuring the Impact of Terrorism." Institute for Economics & Peace, 2023.

     https://www.visionofhumanity.org/global-terrorism-index/

Sources on Social and Economic Impacts

12. **OECD (Organization for Economic Co-operation and Development)**

   - "The Economic Impact of Migration: Why Migration Matters." OECD, 2019.

     https://www.oecd.org/migration/economic-impact-migration.htm

13. **The World Bank**

   - "Forced Displacement and Development." World Bank, 2021.

     https://www.worldbank.org/en/topic/forced-displacement

14. **Amnesty International**

   - "The Human Cost of Immigration Detention." Amnesty International, 2022.

Suggested Reading and Documentaries

16. **Documentary: "Exodus: Our Journey to Europe"**

- A BBC documentary series following the journeys of refugees and migrants as they make their way to Europe.

  https://www.bbc.co.uk/programmes/b07ky7sn

17. **Documentary: "4.1 Miles"**

- A New York Times Op-Docs film capturing the experiences of refugees crossing the Aegean Sea.

Note to the Reader

The sources listed here provide context, analysis, and data that helped shape the discussions in this book. For deeper exploration into specific topics, readers are encouraged to visit the websites and consult the books mentioned. Given the fluid nature of migration and sociopolitical issues, it is recommended that readers refer to the latest editions or updated reports for the most current information.

* 9 7 9 8 3 0 0 1 8 7 1 8 7 *